PRAISE FOR
IN GOD I TRUST

"*In God I Trust* is the perfect book for such a time as this in the United States of America! It carefully explains the unbroken lineage of our national motto while diligently guiding the reader through a journey to make that motto personal. As we celebrate our great nation's 250th birthday, it fervently points us back to a spirit of national dependency and personal reliance on the Lord our God. Especially during this semiquincentennial year, every American should read these words of history and spiritual direction while determining to make the national motto our own personal declaration."

Jerry Boykin, Lieutenant General (ret)
Executive Vice President, Family Research Council

"What's true about leadership in organizational life is equally true in one's personal life: The most difficult person you'll ever have to lead is yourself. While this truth has major implications for institutions large and small in every corner of our country, its force extends well beyond the personal to the national level as 'we the people' play our individual parts to create the common good. *In God I Trust* is a welcome reminder that 'we' is nothing more than the collection of every last 'I.' In other words, the best thing I can do to strengthen our 'we' is to look in the mirror and start with me. Trust me, there can be no better anniversary gift to this great Nation than that. Better yet, trust God."

Dr. Dondi E. Costin, Major General (ret)
United States Air Force – President, Liberty University

"*In God I Trust* is a timely and compelling call to recover the spiritual roots that shaped America's past and can still guide our future. Combining real historical insight with heartfelt pastoral encouragement, General Teichert and Pastor Wells remind us why our national motto cannot simply remain printed on currency, but must be written on the heart. This book invites every reader not only to understand the trust of our founders, but to experience that same personal trust in God today.

Few books speak so clearly to both America's story and America's soul. *In God I Trust* reminds us that the motto engraved on our coins was always meant to be engraved in our lives. A needed and inspiring read for anyone longing for national renewal and personal faith."

Dr. Ben Graham
Director of Faith, Department of the Interior

"The Bible says in Matthew 12:34, 'out of the abundance of the heart, the mouth speaketh.' *In God I Trust* is written by two of the best 'hearts' that I know.

Both Pastor Brad Wells and General John Teichert highlight vital issues that encourage every reader to rediscover the Biblical heritage upon which our nation was founded. From George Washington's calls to prayer, to reminders of Bible verses carved in stone, the truth of our nation's Biblical beginnings is evident.

While living in a culture that desires to tear down the fabric of America's Christian heritage, my dear friends General Teichert and Pastor Wells have developed an exceptional book that characterizes and identifies specific examples of God's designed plan for America.

I am so thankful for this book and encourage everyone to get a copy. The information it entails is so very important as a reminder of our duty to God and country."

Dr. David Gibbs
Founder, Christian Law Association

"Drawing on powerful historical and personal examples, Pastor Brad Wells and General John Teichert remind Americans that *In God We Trust* is more than a motto – it is a guiding principle. As our nation approaches its 250th anniversary, this book calls each of us to declare 'In God I Trust!' and to seek national renewal beginning with personal conviction, humility, and prayer. It is our foundation and it must be our future!"

Congresswoman Cathy McMorris Rodgers
WA-05, 2005-2025

"My dear brothers in the Lord, John Teichert and Brad Wells, have penned an eloquent and entertaining examination of why 'In God We Trust' is woven into the fabric of our nation's 250th birthday celebration. They weave together American history and biblical application to boldly defend the idea that the cause of our Republic is just and therefore our motto as a nation and a people must be made personal."

Todd Starnes
Newsmax host

"John & I know speed! He knows it in the air & I know it on the ground. Our nation & most people in it are always on the go. *In God I Trust* is a great way to intentionally slow our pace so that we can focus in on our personal relationship with Christ. It's in those moments of visiting the Christian scriptures and choosing to pray for our nation & trust in God that we realize how valuable that time really is. It's the power that changes us & ultimately changes not just our nation but the world."

Terry Borcheller
Professional Sportscar Racing Driver & Motorsports Ministries president & chaplain.

"My friends, Brigadier General John Teichert and Pastor Brad Wells, have written a much national needed reminder with their new book, *In God I Trust: Making Our National Motto My Personal Declaration.*

Far too many people in our nation are unaware of our rich history and the irreplaceable role God has played in our nation's 250 years. In addition to that, our culture and even many in our educational systems teach and uphold a victimhood mentality that emphasizes the negativity in life instead of God's direction from Romans 8:28 and the preeminence of His plan and His will in our lives. We each need to reset and rededicate our lives to seeking God's will and that means we take full responsibility for our actions and tell God, I trust YOU for my life's plans. Thanks to two heroes in our nation for reigniting this vital foundational aspect of America's success – it is THE way back for our nation. IN GOD I TRUST!!

Chad Connelly
Founder and President, Faith Wins

"In some ways, our world feels smaller than ever, and there is increasing talk of being 'citizens of the world.' Yet America was built on enduring ideals and on the conviction that we hold certain truths to be self-evident.

'In God We Trust' has long been our national motto, but as retired General John Teichert and Pastor Brad Wells remind us, trust in God must be personal if our faith is to flourish – not only as a nation, but in our individual lives. Freedom, too, becomes meaningful and lasting only when it is personal and when each of us truly puts our trust in God."

Steve Amerson
Award-winning Singer, Songwriter & Recording Artist

"Men and women of character, competence, and courage did something 250 years ago that had never been done – they forged a new nation built on Godly principles. Each generation has defended and built on that sure foundation. Now is our time to ensure the freest, most prosperous nation in the world continues. Two of our nation's current leaders have gifted us with this treasure which dispels secular myths, unlocks the truths of America's greatness, and reveals the key to personal success. I highly recommend this book for skeptic and patriot alike. You'll be empowered and inspired by the truths contained on every page."

Congresswoman Vicky Hartzler
MO-04, 2011-2023
Chair, Bipartisan U.S. Commission on International Religious Freedom

"*In God I Trust* is a timely and compelling work from two men whose lives embody the very truth they proclaim. Brigadier General John "Dragon" Teichert and Pastor Brad Wells write not as detached observers of history, but as faithful servants of God and country, men whose lives reflect integrity, humility, and courageous faith. Drawing from decades of distinguished military leadership and faithful pastoral ministry, they offer a rare and powerful fusion of personal credibility, moral clarity, and spiritual conviction. With bold purpose and biblical precision, they trace the enduring legacy of trust in God that has shaped our national identity and demonstrate why that same trust must once again anchor our personal lives and public conscience. *In God I Trust* is a stirring and urgent call that will inspire each reader to make our national motto their personal declaration."

Captain William L. Miller
Chaplain, USAF

IN GOD I TRUST

MAKING OUR NATIONAL MOTTO MY PERSONAL DECLARATION

JOHN "DRAGON" TEICHERT
U.S. AIR FORCE BRIGADIER GENERAL (RET)

BRAD WELLS
PASTOR, GRACEWAY BAPTIST CHURCH, D.C.

Editor: Jessica Marshall – jessiejmarshall@gmail.com

Publisher: Capital Leadership Books

ISBN: 979-8-234-01142-8 (paperback)

ISBN: 979-8-234-00370-6 (ebook)

TABLE OF CONTENTS

A PERSONAL DECLARATION THAT PROLONGS

THE SCAM OF SEPARATION AND THE NOISE ABOUT NATIONALISM

CONCLUSION

ENSHRINED

BY JOHN TEICHERT

On March 3, 1865, Congress passed a bill requiring the words "In God We Trust" be engraved on all gold and silver coins. It was the last bill that President Abraham Lincoln signed into law before his assassination. Though this slogan had been engraved on some U.S. coins before that time, it was this federal act that first enshrined an acknowledgment of the need for trusting in God into nationwide law.

Yet it was well before that point that trusting God had been enshrined into the fabric of the United States of America. Several decades before, on the morning of September 14, 1814, those who woke up in the city of Baltimore were unsure of what they would see as they looked toward Fort McHenry. That fort, located at a strategic position which played a pivotal role in keeping the British out of Baltimore's inner harbor, had been under heavy attack for over 24 hours from the guns of powerful British warships. Only 25 years removed from birth under the Constitution, engulfed in a battle for national survival, Baltimore's citizens awoke on that morning to a beautiful sight – the American flag was still waving over Fort McHenry. While the soldiers therein were battle-weary, they had not been defeated.

Francis Scott Key, detained during those days on a British warship, saw the same glorious sight on that tumultuous morning. The flag waving over Fort McHenry inspired him to pen the words of our National Anthem. The following stanza was a key part of his thoughts on that late summer morning in Charm City:

Oh! thus be it ever, when freemen shall stand
Between their loved homes and the war's desolation!
Blest with victory and peace, may the heaven-rescued land
Praise the Power that hath made and preserved us a nation.
Then conquer we must, when our cause it is just,
And this be our motto: "In God is our trust."
And the star-spangled banner in triumph shall wave
O'er the land of the free and the home of the brave!

The words of what would become our National Anthem were soon distributed to a population who already understood that they were citizens of a heaven-rescued land. Only a generation had passed since the nation's founding, and they recognized that the Lord was the Power that had made and preserved them a nation. Trust in Him was enshrined in their culture.

A few decades before the War of 1812, 56 men gathered in Philadelphia to sign the nation's Declaration of Independence. It was a bold act from these courageous visionaries in which they risked everything. To punctuate their thoughts in this incredible document, they revealed the source of their confidence in taking such a treasonous step: "And for the support of this Declaration, with a firm reliance on the protection of divine Providence, we mutually pledge to each other our Lives, our Fortunes and our sacred Honor." As they put everything on the line – their lives, their fortunes, and their sacred honor – they demonstrated something powerful. They weren't relying on themselves: their skills, their education, their knowledge, or their courage. Instead, they were firmly relying on the protection of divine Providence. In God We Trust was already enshrined in their basic principles.

These leaders were able to enshrine In God We Trust into the nation's law, culture, and principles because it was already enshrined in Christian theology. In a Biblically literate society, they had read about and understood the trustworthiness of God as revealed in His Word. They knew, for example, the Psalmist's threefold plea: "O Israel, trust thou in the LORD: he is their help and their shield. O house of Aaron, trust in the LORD: he is their help and their shield. Ye that fear the LORD, trust in the LORD: he is their help and their shield" (Psalm 115:9-11).

When God said something once, America's Founders knew to believe it. But when He said something back-to-back-to-back, then they knew it should be on the forefront of their minds. What's more, they knew it was well worthy of engraving onto those things that would fill every pocket and populate every wallet.

In 1865, there was some debate about engraving "In God We Trust" on every coin. There were those who thought that such a phrase was inappropriate. Curiously, it wasn't because they were secular humanists who strove to purge every mention of God from their society. Just the opposite. They simply had a better alternative: "In God Alone Is Our Trust." This group wanted to emphasize that God was not just to be trusted as prominent, but instead as the preeminent. He wasn't just to be highly trusted but ultimately trusted.

While it was the shorter and catchier motto that was signed into law, the more powerful intent has been enshrined into the fabric of American society. It was relevant in 1776, 1814, 1865, and it's relevant today!

In God We Trust!

This is a book about the United States of America that follows the unbroken national lineage of that motto. But it doesn't stop there! It's also a spiritual journey that is designed to make the motto personal.

In God I Trust!

It provides the pathway to transform the understanding of our national motto into our personal declaration. It carefully illuminates the pathway of national dependency and personal reliance. It is not just academic history. It is individual hierarchy. And God must be at the top!

I am honored to be joined in bringing this concept to life by my Pastor. His portions are intentionally and powerfully pastoral, and he astutely guides the reader toward the applicability of the history that I prioritize in my portions.

We start with a section that describes the related words that are essential elements of the journey – faith, belief, and trust. The next section describes the trust in God that is inseparably grafted into our founding, followed by one that briefly highlights the consistent application of national trust that has flowed from the headwaters of our history. The fourth section transitions the message to the personal level, providing practical actions to turn national history into personal destiny. No work of this type would be complete without a section on the triggering topics of our age, including separation of church and state and Christian nationalism, tackled in our final section. We acknowledge the diverse religious traditions of our Founders, but are also firmly convinced that Christianity and Biblical literacy played an oversized role in the culture in which they lived. In the conclusion, we each punctuate our claims one last time.

In God I Trust is woven together to celebrate our nation's 250th birthday while highlighting the threads that lead towards national and personal revival.

Each chapter is written by one of us, as noted at the beginning of each, so that the reader will know the perspective of the words contained therein. But the message is consistent throughout … In God We Trust … In God I Trust.

It's long past time to make our national motto our personal declaration!

INTRODUCTION II

A PASTORAL PERSPECTIVE

BY BRAD WELLS

"You will never be over what's under you until you are under what's over you."

I was a young man when I first heard this quote by the late Dr. Adrian Rogers. It underscores the truth that submission *to* God is the key to power *with* God.

Immediately, I see Jacob wrestling with God, unwilling to let Him go until he receives the desired blessing. In the process, his name was changed to "Israel," meaning "he who struggles and prevails with God."

Jacob was wounded in the struggle. The angel touched the hollow of his thigh, giving him a limp for the rest of his life.

In the moment, what did that scenario look like? It looked like a desperate man, clinging with all his strength to the Only One who could bless him. Only *under God* would he prevail. Only *under God* would he proceed.

As I write, our beloved United States of America is in a battle for the blessing of God. Some would say the struggle is not worth the blessing.

Some would remove *under God* from our pledge and *In God We Trust* from our currency.

Jacob struggled with God and is eternally blessed.

This is our choice: will God prevail or will self? Will we submit to dependence under God, or strive for independence out from under Him?

As for me and my house, we choose the God of our fathers of faith, who is also the God of the Founding Fathers of our nation. We will continue in the struggle, through prayer and fasting, to "lay hold" on the blessing of God upon our nation. We will readily acknowledge our position under His sovereign authority.

Until His soon return, it is *only* IN GOD WE TRUST.

SECTION 1

THE ESSENTIAL INTERPLAY BETWEEN BELIEF, FAITH, AND TRUST

CHAPTER 1

TAKING THE FIRST STEP ON THE JOURNEY OF TRUST

BY BRAD WELLS

When I was eighteen years of age, my parents surrendered to go to Papua New Guinea as missionaries. My dad, Dennis Wells, asked me to put my plans to study business on hold for a year and join him, my mom, and my two younger brothers in the adventure of beginning anew on a tropical island.

(A year turned into a 20-year calling, but that's another story.)

We moved to the highlands region and took up residence in a thatched-roof hut six hours from the supply town of Mt. Hagen in a village named Palapini. Ours was the last village on the north side of the Polu River. Across the river were many more villages in need of supplies, education, and, most importantly, the Word of God. There was no question: we were crossing that river.

There were two ways across it. We could trek (more like *slide*) down a steep muddy 20-foot embankment, swim across, and climb back up the other side. Or we could use the vine-suspension bridge made of jungle materials and fastened to trees on either side of the gorge.

We boys had no problem placing our feet on the single foot-vine and holding onto the attached hand-vines on either side, crossing much like a tightrope walker with training wires. As any teenager would, we reveled in the rush of risk.

My dear mother, however, found no joy in the proposition. I vividly remember the first time she came to that bridge. She stood on the bank holding the hand-vines, with one foot on the foot-vine, petrified to abandon *terra firma* and place her second foot onto the bridge.

When she finally did have both feet on the bridge, she began looking down at her feet, preparing to take the next step, and the bridge began to swing. The more she tried to perfect her next step by looking down and placing her foot just right, the more the bridge swung. The more the bridge swung, the more off balance she became, the harder it was to take another step, and the more terrified she grew.

I can still hear her voice. "Den," she cried out in panic. "The bridge is swinging. I don't know if I can do this!"

"Dee!" Dad shouted from the other side of the river. "Don't look down! Look at me. The bridge will hold you. Your foot will find its balance on the vine. Just take the next step. Keep your body weight going forward and you will fall into rhythm with the bridge."

The strength in his voice and the closing gap between them worked a miracle in her and, step by step, she grew more confident, eventually reaching the other side of her great trial of faith.

Let's make this personal.

You have come to a crossing on *your* journey of faith. The bridge represents the faith it will take to reach the next milestone.

I can see you standing there looking at it right now. You know God has asked you to do something. What is it? Is it to talk to your coworker about the Lord, attempt a new task, fill out an application, commit to marry that girl?

Faith is a given. It's a gift. It's where we start with God. Ephesians 2:8 says, "For by grace are ye saved through faith: and *that not of yourselves: it is the gift of God* (emphasis always mine)." Romans 12:3 says God has "dealt to every man a *measure* of faith." Whatever God is asking of you, He has already given you the faith to do it.

If you have not yet repented and believed in Jesus Christ, God has given you enough faith to do so. Galatians 2:16 says we are not justified (made right with God) by works, but by "the faith of Jesus Christ." It is His faith – He thought it up. He paid for it with His blood. And He gave you enough of it to take the step you must take to cross that Bridge when you come to it.

The faith is not only already given, but it is also bursting to activate! Romans 10:8-9 says, "The word is nigh thee, even in thy *mouth*, and in thy *heart*: that is, the *word of faith* which we preach; That if thou shalt confess with thy mouth the Lord Jesus, and shalt believe in thine heart that God hath raised him from the dead, thou shalt be saved."

Perhaps you are already born again by faith, and you are now looking at the next bridge of baptism. Don't worry, the bridge will hold you and you will not drown in that baptismal pool! You will find all the strength you need is available to publicly proclaim your faith in Jesus Christ.

Maybe your "bridge of faith" is a new opportunity, or a new surrender, or a new relationship. Do not shrink in fear on the far side of God's will. Your faith needs to grow! The disciples said, "Lord, *increase* our faith" (Luke 17:5). The chasm may seem deeper, and the bank may seem farther, but God always gives enough faith to get you successfully across.

Secondly, let's look at another word that comes immediately on the heels of faith: *belief.*

Belief has an intellectual ring to it. You cannot truly believe something unless you know something about it. In our illustration, the fact that Dad had made it to the other side was enough evidence for Mom to know she could as well. She simply needed to believe it *and move forward.*

Oh! But the "devils believe and tremble" (James 2:9). Intellectual belief is not enough. Mom could've stood trembling all day long on the north side of the river, seeing Dad on the other side, believing the bridge could hold her just as well, but never acting on her faith.

So, let me rephrase that: *Saving* belief is focusing on the *truth* enough to put all your weight on the bridge of faith. It's agreeing that the chair can hold you and actually releasing your body into it. It is knowing a parachute can save you and thrusting yourself out of the airplane.

Belief is the first step *onto* faith. It is beginning in obedience. Romans 1:5 says, "By whom (speaking of Jesus) we have received grace (there's that gift wrapped in faith again!) . . . for *obedience* to the faith among all nations, for His name." Paul goes on to say in chapter 6 and verse 17, "But God be thanked . . . ye have *obeyed* from the heart that form of doctrine which was delivered you."

Let me backtrack for a moment: Faith is a gift from God. But when is it given? Well, Romans 10:17 says, "So then faith cometh by hearing, and hearing by the Word of God."

Back in the village, we had heard there was a bridge that would take us across the River Polu. Sure enough, when we came around the last bend of the jungle trail leading up to it, there it was.

In a similar way, when we *hear* the Word or the *truth*, we are offered faith freely. Now we can choose to believe its claims or choose to doubt. If we continue to doubt the truth of faith, we will shrivel and die on the bank of fear.

This is why we must actively believe! Take the step. God has promised if we *do* these things, we will never fall: "Wherefore the rather, brethren, give diligence to make your calling and election sure: for if ye *do* these things, ye shall never fall" (2 Peter 1:10).

This brings us to our third word: *trust.*

If you look it up in the dictionary *trust* means a "firm belief." I see a continuum of faith *and* obedience in that definition.

Trust is looking back at the last step, realizing what God said was true, and *continuing to move forward.*

TRUSTING THE LAWS OF FAITH

It was a warm, wet afternoon, not much over 70 degrees, when we took off from Mt. Hagen's Kagamuga Airport on this particularly cloudy Monday morning. We perpetually felt as if we had just stepped out of the shower.

Long six-pocket cargo pants hung heavy with tools off my hips, a short-sleeved tropical shirt loosely covering my thin frame. Mud-smudged boots and an Aussie outback-style hat completed my headed-for-the-bush outfit.

The two-hour flight on a single-engine Cessna 182 took us over endless patches of thick green, broccoli-shaped hills. Crags of mountain peaks jutted up here and there, cutting through the triple canopy forest to an altitude of 12,000, even 14,000 feet.

Headed for Owena, a mission station on the top of a mountain in Southern Highlands, my sixteen-year-old kid brother, Chad, sat next to me, chattering away about the last flight he had taken in his aviation training.

"Now, boys," the missionary pilot's voice crackled over our headsets, arresting our attention. "We're getting close to the runway. You see that mountain ahead of us?"

Chad and I muttered our acknowledgment of the tiny patch of dirt we could barely make out.

"The runway is right at the edge of that cliff. At this time of day, if I come at it level, the thermal air pockets may push us up too far and I won't be able to land the plane on the short airstrip. I *usually* have to fly right at the cliff and trust the thermals to lift us just in time to set our wheels on that runway. I am going to do a flyby and see what the air is doing today. OK?"

Usually? I was suddenly riveted to the pilot's revelation, one that had not been a part of the initial briefing.

"OK. Whatever you say, sir," Chad and I tried to sound confident.

We felt the thermals alright, making our stomachs weak as we bumped upward with an out-of-control motion.

"Yep! We've got a pocket, boys," he shouted in our ears. "Here we go around again. This time, it will look as if we are going to crash until the very last second. You're going to have to trust me now, ya hear?"

It seemed all the water in my mouth suddenly popped out on my forehead.

"Sure," I mustered through my tight chest. "We trust you."

We flew, what looked like, straight at the cliff, about ten feet below its ledge. Closer and closer, with no sign of lift.

Then, right at the last second, the little craft suddenly lurched upward, and we were two feet above the hard-packed earthen runway.

"There we are, boys!" The pilot laughed delightedly. "See, what I told ya? You have to trust the air!"

And I did, as the ground rumbled beneath us.

Belief is the knowledge that thermal air pockets are there and will act in a certain way.

Faith – that is *effective, saving faith* – begins by flying towards the cliff.

Trust is the willingness to *continue* flying at the face of death until the Creator of the air and all of its laws lifts you to safety!

Trust is my mom taking her eyes *off her feet* and looking at my dad, listening to his voice, and continuing to step across the bridge as the river rushed beneath her.

We have heard that courage is not the absence of fear, but the ability to press forward despite fear. Trust is the courage to *continue believing* in the heat of the trial.

In God I Trust.

These three words, *faith*, *belief*, and *trust* make up a synergistic cycle that compels us to confidently make our national motto our *personal declaration.*

We all must decide: will we shrink and shrivel on the banks of doubt? Or will we believe the truth and take a step . . . and then another . . . and then another . . .

Years after my mother's crossing, I brought my new bride to visit my parents in Papua New Guinea. I had returned to the States to attend Bible college instead of business college. I had heard the call myself to become a missionary. I had met and married my life's partner, Deborah. And now we were surveying the mission field in a new light – as a married couple, yoked together to reach the world for Christ.

You guessed it. One of the first places I took her when we reached our remote village was the vine-suspension bridge over the River Polu.

The cycle of faith, belief, and trust had begun for *my* family.

CHAPTER 2

TEICHERT'S TAKE ON TRUST

BY JOHN TEICHERT

The Hall of Fame of Faith is a compelling section of scripture. From the beginning of Hebrews 11, it is clear that God's priority is the faithfulness of His people. By our faith, God is able to bring about His perfect plan through us. And "without faith it is impossible to please him: for he that cometh to God must believe that he is, and that he is a rewarder of them that diligently seek him" (Hebrews 11:6).

But, it becomes clear at the breakpoint of verse 35 that faithfulness doesn't necessarily result in temporal success. Sometimes faith allows believers to subdue kingdoms, work righteousness, obtain promises, stop the mouths of lions, quench the violence of fire, escape the edge of the sword, be made strong, wax valiant in fight, turn to flight the armies of the aliens, and receive dead raised to life again. Yet, in other cases faith results in torture, mocking, scourging, imprisonment, stoning, dismemberment, temptation, murder, poverty, affliction, torment, and disorientation.

God focuses on our faithfulness. That is what is in our control.

The results are fully left up to Him and they are solidly His business.

Acknowledging that important truth is the core of what begins to transform belief and faith into trust.

The book of Romans expounds upon this important truth about the nature of trust. God is ever willing and imminently able to fulfill His plan, and the Christian must step forward in faith and trust because "we know that all things work together for good to them that love God, to them who are the called according to his purpose" (Romans 8:28). Even when our role in that plan may face looming challenges and daunting hardships, we "reckon that the sufferings of this present time are not worthy to be compared with the glory which shall be revealed in us" (Romans 8:18).

Our Biblical and national Founders translated their trust in God into bold action because they embraced these truths. The Hebrew children did the same as they faced the fiery furnace, Esther did so as she prepared herself to approach the king, and the signers of the Declaration of Independence did the same as they signed their names to our founding document with a firm reliance on the protection of divine Providence.

DAUNTING DECISIONS FOR ALL OF US

High-level leaders face challenges that we can only imagine. These challenges are made even more daunting when they trust in their own wisdom instead of trusting in God. Solomon recognized his insufficiency and the need to turn to God in trust: "Give therefore thy servant an understanding heart to judge thy people, that I may discern between good and bad: for who is able to judge this thy so great a people?" (I Kings 3:9). His willingness to turn to the Lord for wisdom and discernment "pleased the Lord" (I Kings 3:10) while giving Solomon an unmatched ability to discern, understand, and apply wisdom.

Senate Chaplain of the late 1940s, Peter Marshall, recognized this same important truth as he prayed:

> *We need Thy strength, Thy guidance, Thy wisdom. There are problems far greater than any wisdom of man can solve. What shall our leaders do in such an hour?*

May Thy wisdom and Thy power come upon the President of these United States, the Senators and Congressmen, to whom have been entrusted leadership. May the responsibility lie heavily on their hearts, until they are ready to acknowledge their helplessness and turn to Thee. Give to them the honesty, the courage, and the moral integrity to confess that they don't know what to do. Only then can they lead us as a nation beyond human wisdom to Thee, who alone hast the answer.

A few years before Chaplain Marshall graced the chambers of the U.S. Senate, President Franklin Delano Roosevelt passed away on April 12, 1945 during his fourth term and at the climax of World War II. Three days later he was buried, and the day after that, newly sworn-in President Harry S. Truman stood in front of a joint session of Congress.

Throughout his speech, President Truman called for the need and the necessity of Divine guidance. He closed the speech with these thoughts:

At this moment, I have in my heart a prayer. As I have assumed my heavy duties, I humbly pray Almighty God, in the words of King Solomon: 'Give therefore thy servant an understanding heart to judge thy people, that I may discern between good and bad; for who is able to judge this thy so great a people?' I ask only to be a good and faithful servant of my Lord and my people.

It was said of this speech that:

Truman had but a fraction of FDR's gift for oratory, but his voice was steady and firm. For twelve years the president who addressed the world from this pulpit spoke in the intonations of the moneyed East Coast establishment. This voice was different. It was the voice of a common man, asking God for guidance, and the response was the loudest affirmation Truman's ears had ever encountered.

Experts have said that "the first four months of his administration should rank as the most challenging and action-packed of any four-month period in any American presidency." Truman certainly needed the understanding heart that topped King Solomon's prayer list. The new president knew that his duties demanded a preeminent trust in God.

While such a trusting spirit is critical for our nation's leaders, it is also essential for each one of us. Human behavior experts estimate that the average human makes 35,000 decisions a day. Many of them are small, but some of them are substantial. And even the small ones, taken together, create the basis for character that informs everything about our lives.

That's why we need trusting wisdom. It is why we need an understanding heart. It is why we need to be able to properly discern between good and bad. It is why we need to be able to judge. It is why we need understanding.

And God is pleased when we ask for these things. He offers them freely and liberally – "If any of you lack wisdom, let him ask of God, that giveth to all men liberally, and upbraideth not; and it shall be given him" (James 1:5). They are far more important than wealth, or victory, or longevity. In fact, wisdom, discernment, understanding, and judgment form a reliable foundation for these more temporal benefits.

35,000 decisions!

Just the daunting nature of such scope and scale of decision making should drive us to our knees. It should expose our understand our desperate need for the Lord's guidance and prompt daily prayer and Bible reading. Everything else builds upon the foundation we create, and it all begins with trust. Not just a collective trust, but an individual trust – In God I Trust!

ALL OTHERS MUST BRING DATA

During my first military assignment in the Pentagon, my boss was ultimately responsible for all acquisition programs in the Department of Defense. As one would expect, he was a very analytical man who took this massive responsibility seriously. After all, his daily decisions affected billions of dollars and the future of American weaponry. So, he hung a sign outside his office that said: "In God we trust, all others must bring Data."

Indeed, in God we should trust. We should trust Him for our daily mundane decisions as much as we should trust Him for grandiose strategic decisions. We should trust Him during the difficult times as much as we should trust Him during the good times. We should trust Him as much in 2026 as our Founders trusted him in 1776. We should trust Him when we are surrounded by those who doubt as much as we should trust Him when we are surrounded by those who believe. We should trust Him when we are facing a godless culture as much as we should trust Him when we are in the relative safety of the church house. At all times, in all situations, and through all circumstances we must say … In God We Trust … In God I Trust … All others must bring data!

Yet despite our national motto, we have flipped the logic of trust on its head. Our situation is reminiscent of the Israelites as they wandered in the wilderness: "They have turned aside quickly out of the way which I commanded them: they have made them a molten calf, and have worshipped it, and have sacrificed thereunto, and said, These be thy gods, O Israel, which have brought thee up out of the land of Egypt" (Exodus 32:8).

In today's America we trust in everything but God. Today, it is the Lord who must bring data to be trusted by a society who has made itself an array of molten calves in which to trust. It is these calves that we errantly credit for the positive qualities of our society. It is these calves that we worship. It is these calves unto which we sacrifice. Our twisted memories reason that *these be the gods which have brought us up out of our Egypt.* In doing so, we have turned aside from the way that God commanded us.

Today, we trust in the calves of prosperity. We trust in the calves of education. We trust in the calves of globalization. We trust in the calves of nationalism. We trust in the calves of tolerance. We trust in the calves of reason. We trust in the calves of power and political affiliation.

In today's American society, we trust in the calves of man's philosophy. We trust in the calves of a living Constitution. We trust in the calves of a progressive mindset. We trust in the calves of unbounded gratification. We trust in the calves of a secular morality. We trust in the calves of an accommodating doctrine.

We must burn these calves in the fire and return to the One who is worthy of our trust.

HORSES, CHARIOTS, F-22S, AND PILLARS OF SUCCESS

While we should deeply appreciate their service and sacrifice, Americans should never be lulled into thinking that the brave men and women who serve in the military are America's ultimate source of security. The United States is not great because of military strength, diplomatic sway, nor economic supremacy. It is not great because of geographic separation nor resource superiority. We are only a great nation when we remember that the Lord is our true source of greatness.

After several hundred hours in her cockpit, I can personally testify that the F-22 Raptor is an amazing machine. It is a grand flying chariot propelled by unmatched horsepower. Even with its dominant characteristics, our nation must not trust in it to secure us apart from the Lord. Nor should we do so because of a portfolio of Abrams tanks, a fleet of aircraft carriers, or an arsenal of nuclear weapons. We must trust in the Ultimate Source who is ultimately trustworthy.

Psalm 20:7 has been my theme verse from the earliest days of my Christian life (I was saved at age 32): "Some trust in chariots, and some in horses: but we will remember the name of the LORD our God." It is a great reminder to me that the real source of power, protection, peace and provision comes from the Lord and not through the mightiest machines made by man. I often included this verse next to my name as I signed pictures of F-22 Raptors when I had the opportunity to fly these amazing modern-day horses and chariots during the early days of the program as a test pilot.

The book of Exodus provides an amazing contrast between trusting in the Lord and trusting in societal symbols of prestige.

In their escape from Egypt, the faithful followed God's guidance – His pillar of cloud by day and His pillar of fire by night. The Egyptians, on the other hand, pursued with ungodly reliance on their secular strength. While those symbols of earthly potency were quick in their pursuits, they were rapidly overwhelmed by the waters of the Red Sea at the command of the Lord our God. This situation provides a powerful punctuation of the truths of Psalm 20:7.

Today, may we follow God's guidance – His proverbial pillar of cloud by day and pillar of fire by night. While the world around us is relying on their secular strength, may we unfailingly remember the name of the Lord our God. Chariots and horses of all forms can be rapidly overwhelmed and overthrown by Providential waters.

On July 4, 1776, in addition to unanimously adopting the Declaration of Independence, the Continental Congress formed a committee consisting of Benjamin Franklin, Thomas Jefferson, and John Adams to design the seal of our newly declared independent nation. Their designs were ultimately tabled, with a completely new design finally adopted in 1782.

Yet, their drafts powerfully reveal the Biblically minded thoughts that dominated the founder's motivations and perspectives about independence.

Franklin's draft displayed images of Moses and God's people in safety on the far side of the Red Sea, with Pharaoh and his men being overwhelmed by the waters. A pillar of fire is central to this design, designating the source of power and strength for God's people. His recommended motto: Rebellion to Tyrants is Obedience to God.

Jefferson created a draft with a similar theme, displaying the children of Israel in the Wilderness. In his depiction, they were led by a pillar of cloud by day and a pillar of fire by night, demonstrating a powerful analogue to Exodus 13:21-22: "And the LORD went before them by day in a pillar of a cloud, to lead them the way; and by night in a pillar of fire, to give them light; to go by day and night: He took not away the pillar of the cloud by day, nor the pillar of fire by night, from before the people."

Our Founders saw their departure from British rule as an analogue of the Israelites flight from Egypt. This nation's deliverance and ultimate success would be guided by trusting in God's direction, day and night.

Today, our ultimate success depends upon the same – it is the pillar of our success. May we never forget it!

SECTION 2

A NATIONAL FOUNDATION OF TRUST

CHAPTER 3

BUILDING ON A CLEAN FOUNDATION

BY BRAD WELLS

"In God We Trust" did not become our national motto until 1956 when, by a joint resolution of Congress, President Dwight D. Eisenhower signed it into law. Yet, as we will undeniably prove, it was both the foundation and framework from which our Founding Fathers built our great nation.

I am going to give way to my coauthor, trusted friend, and colleague General John Teichert to rigorously describe this truth. But from a pastoral perspective, let me begin this section with the words of another head of government who built his nation of trust in God.

Weathered and wise from battle, King David runs his thumb over the strings of his harp, pausing to allow his fingers to find a chord, and begins singing, "Unto Thee, O LORD, do I lift up my soul" (Psalm 25:1).

(I think he was a baritone, but to each his own.)

To whom was David singing? *Unto Thee, O YHWH*, the unpronounceable name of God. The Eternal, Self-Existing One. It is translated as "LORD" 6,510 times in the King James Version.

"The LORD, The LORD God, merciful and gracious, long-suffering, and abundant in goodness and truth" (Exodus 34:6).

"The LORD, the Lord of all the earth" (Joshua 3:13).

"The LORD, the LORD . . . a deliverer" (Judges 3:9, 15).

"The Lord, the LORD of hosts, the mighty One of Israel" (Isaiah 1:24).

"Who is like unto Thee, O LORD, among the gods? Who is like Thee, glorious in holiness, fearful in praises, doing wonders?" (Exodus 15:11)

"Who is like unto the LORD our God, who dwelleth on high, Who humbleth himself to behold the things that are in heaven, and in the earth!" (Psalm 113:5-6)

And in 6,502 other instances, the grandeur and mighty power of our LORD God is described!

As we acknowledge His character, we can only worship. He is the *source* of all power. He is the giver of all good and perfect gifts. He is the light we must seek in order to walk in truth.

This is THE LORD to whom David would dare say, *Unto Thee, O LORD, do I lift up my soul.*

Now we see David laying aside his harp, perhaps kneeling, but most certainly lifting up his hands to the heavens. Lifting them as if holding something very precious in their palms.

Indeed, it is his most precious possession, his very soul!

Take a moment and act out David's metaphor. Right now, find a quiet spot, and lift up your soul with your hands towards the heavens.

If you think this is an extraordinary exercise, consider the prophet Jeremiah's admonition, "Let us lift up our heart with our hands unto God in the heavens" (Lamentations 3:41).

David unashamedly lifts up his *soul*. The whole of his mind, his will, and his emotions. All he divines, decides, and desires is held upward to the Almighty Creator of heaven and earth.

As you continue holding up your soul – all you think, all you want, and all you feel – what posture does your soul take?

I must say, when I literally lift up my soul to God, one word that comes to mind is *vulnerable*. I am expressing complete dependence upon His acceptance and not another's. I feel totally exposed before my God.

It's rather intimidating, isn't it?

Here in our nation's capital, I have been appointed as a volunteer chaplain of the House of Representatives. This means I regularly walk among the most powerful people on the planet. I bet you could guess what my greatest problem in this line of work is. Pride.

(And it's yours too, may I add. Every temptation stems from the root of pride; be it pleasure, possessions, or prominence.)

I practice physically lifting up my soul to God often. It helps me tremendously. I find a quiet spot with nearly no one around, and I stand there with my hands uplifted, waiting before the Lord, signaling I am trusting in His power alone.

I remember the admonition, "Humble yourselves therefore under the mighty hand of God, that He may exalt you in due time" (1 Peter 5:6).

Andrew Murray aptly says humility is the "most important duty to God, and the best safeguard for your heart."

When asked how to conquer pride, he emphasizes its simplicity: "Two things are required. Do what God says is *your* work – humble yourself. Trust God for what He says is *His* work – He will lift you up."

God resists the proud. He sets His face against the proud. Not one of us can afford to be proud.

So, as I stand there, in the middle of the Capitol, lifting up my soul to God, another picture enters my mind.

It is that of my wife asking our children if they had washed their hands for supper. "Sure!" They answer too hastily.

"Let me check," was the dreadcd reply.

It was just previously in Psalm 24 that David asks the probing questions, "Who shall ascend into the hill of the LORD? Or who shall stand in His holy place?"

The dreaded answer resounds, "He that hath clean hands, and a pure heart; who hath not lifted up his soul unto vanity, nor sworn deceitfully" (Psalm 24:3-4).

Man! I should've thought of that first before I decided to stand here on this prominent Hill with my hands outstretched requesting power to do His work! Now it's time to kneel.

My friend, are our hands clean? We may stand all day with our hands lifted to heaven and *never* expect to be heard if our hands are dirty.

*Unto Thee, O LORD, **do** I lift up my soul.*

Our hands speak.

What have I *done*? Is my life marked by a spiritual vigilance striving to resist immoral thoughts and deeds?

What have I *trusted?* Have I compromised with the excuse that I'm serving the "greater good"?

What have I *said*? Have I lied to cover up the truth?

You and I are urged to fall on our face in confession *first* before we can ever attempt to lift up our souls.

"Draw nigh to God, and He will draw nigh to you. Cleanse your hands, ye sinners; and purify your hearts, ye double-minded" (James 4:8).

If we are in need of cleansing, the fountain is open! From the depth of our conscience to the extremity of our habits, God desires to purify us.

"If we confess our sins, He is faithful and just to forgive us our sins, and to cleanse us from all unrighteousness" (1 John 1:9).

"How much more shall the blood of Christ, who through the eternal Spirit offered Himself without spot to God, purge your conscience from dead works to serve the living God?" (Hebrews 9:14)

Purified and purged from "dirty" and "dead" works, we now have confidence to serve the living God! The *force* of His power can now freely flow through us.

After just such a time of cleansing and worship, I was asked to stand beside a powerful public servant as he took questions from the press. He pointed to the black leather Bible I always carry and said, "Hold that where people can see it."

Another time, after being asked to preach a short message to a group of congressmen, I was reprimanded by a high-ranking appointee. "When asked to preach," she said in reference to my five-minute challenge, "politely decline." (Wow—I'm guessing she wouldn't appreciate my 45-minute sermon on Sunday either!) The following day I received a call from the leader of that same caucus saying he had been asked to remove me ("kick me out" were his exact words). He would not but wanted me to know I had an adversary.

Well, not *exactly* the one he was thinking of . . .

My point is, neither acceptance nor disapproval from man will inhibit the flow of God's power through us when we humbly lift up our souls with clean hands unto Him.

Here is something I have learned: when I am humble, it doesn't hurt, and I don't hurt anyone else either. I'm just the *course*, not the *source* or the *force*. He can use me as He wills.

When we become the channel, it is no longer about *us*, but only and forever about *Him*.

King David rises from the floor, cleansed and at peace.

He retunes his harp and continues . . .

Unto Thee, O LORD, do I lift up my soul. O, my God, I trust in Thee . . .

CHAPTER 4

THE FAITHFUL FOUNDATIONS OF A NEW NATION

BY JOHN TEICHERT

I am fascinated by American history, especially that which revolves around our nation's founding. I am proud of our national heritage and have no hesitancy in investing my life in service to the United States of America. I first took my oath of office to "support and defend the Constitution of the United States" as a seventeen-year-old young man in Cambridge, Massachusetts as I started Air Force ROTC at MIT. That oath is even more sweet when I remember that I first took it alongside a particularly attractive fellow ROTC cadet who has now been my wife for 28 years.

I grew up in a loving and patriotic family on the northwest tip of the country – Port Angeles, Washington. As an eighth-grade boy in 1986, I went to our small community movie theatre and watched Top Gun. It was then and there that I decided that I wanted to fly fast jets and live a life on the edge of the danger zone. I then did my research about aviation opportunities. The F-15E Strike Eagle was just starting to fly as the newest and best aircraft, and so I decided to join the Air Force.

Throughout my service, I humbly and regularly understood that I was part of a long and unbroken legacy that extended back to those who first set foot on dry ground on our continent.

In our nerdy household, my wife and I playfully argue about whether Issac Newton or Albert Einstein is the greatest scientist of all time. As a PhD quantum chemist and professor at the United States Naval Academy, she favors Einstein. As a fighter pilot – a practitioner of classic physics – I prefer Newton. In this rare case, I'm right and she's wrong. The following Newton quotes about his faith are an important supplement to my evidence when this topic pops up in our home:

"Gravity explains the motions of the planets, but it cannot explain who sets the planets in motion."

"I find more remarks of authenticity in the Bible than in any profane history whatsoever."

"Atheism is so senseless and odious to mankind that it never had many professors."

"He who thinks half-heartedly will not believe in God; but he who really thinks has to believe in God."

Newton is also credited with claiming that the scientific community benefits from "standing on the shoulders of giants." So does the faith community, and so does the United States of America!

Our willingness to look back at the trusting faith of our American predecessors not only allows us to understand the foundation of our society, but it also directs our gaze upward as we look backward. "I will lift up mine eyes unto the hills, from whence cometh my help. My help cometh from the LORD, which made heaven and earth" (Psalm 121:1-2).

Looking back prompts us to lift up our eyes to higher callings, greater purposes, and elevated meaning. Solemn consideration for our predecessors is powerful, poignant, and thought-provoking. Ultimately, it gives us all a chance to consider our mortality, our value, and our purpose in life.

Consider the spiritual testimony of President Abraham Lincoln:

> *When I left home to take this chair of State, I requested my countrymen to pray for me; I was not then a Christian. When my son died, the severest trial of my life, I was not then a Christian. But when I went to Gettysburg, and looked upon the graves of our dead heroes, who had fallen in defence of their country, I then and there consecrated myself to Christ.*

Through these words, President Lincoln is telling us that he accepted Christ because of an overwhelming consideration of the fallen. In an important sense, Lincoln realized he was a dead man beholding other dead men on that field. After all, the Bible tells us that all are dead in trespasses and sin, and are guilty before God (Ephesians 2:1, Romans 3:19-20). A day of memorial had caused Lincoln to lift up his eyes to the hills, and he came to the natural conclusion that his help cometh from the LORD.

It is with reverent humility that we share our past in the pages to follow to direct our nation's gaze upward. And as we do so, may we be reminded of our important trust-filled responsibility from Lincoln's words at Gettysburg: "It is for us the living, rather, to be dedicated here to the unfinished work which they who fought here have thus far so nobly advanced."

STEPPING ONTO DRY GROUND

Veteran's Day, celebrated annually on November 11, allows us to properly pay tribute to those who have served America in our nation's armed forces. It is fitting to recognize them in this way. Yet, there is another group of veterans that we should remember on that day as well. On November 11, 1620, a group of pilgrims found calm within the safety of Cape Cod. They were veterans of a 66-day journey from the old world to the new world, about to step onto dry ground. Before doing so, they drafted and signed what is now known as the Mayflower Compact – our nation's first Constitution. It was a document that bound them together with common purpose, mutual protection, and civil order. The main body of this document stated:

Having undertaken, for the Glory of God, and advancement of the Christian faith and honor of our King and Country, a voyage to plant the first colony in the Northern parts of Virginia, do by these presents, solemnly and mutually, in the presence of God, and one another, covenant and combine ourselves together into a civil body politic; for our better ordering, and preservation and furtherance of the ends aforesaid; and by virtue hereof to enact, constitute, and frame, such just and equal laws, ordinances, acts, constitutions, and offices, from time to time, as shall be thought most meet and convenient for the general good of the colony; unto which we promise all due submission and obedience.

These American forefathers, in the midst of their foundational document, made their purpose clear – bringing glory to God. They were not bashful about declaring that purpose, using those important words as the reliable basis for their society and to carry them successfully through the tough times that they would face in the days ahead. Their focus on such a common purpose allowed them to endure and thrive amidst their challenges.

These trust-filled patriots and pilgrims also had a common mission: the "advancement of the Christian faith." This was not a group of atheists. It was not a group of agnostics. It was not even a group of lackluster Christians.

Instead, it was a group of Bible-believing Christians. These believers were passionate about their faith and were determined to carry it to the ends of the earth. They understood, as should we, that their mission in life was to advance the cause of Christ. By confirming this mission in their foundational document, they covenanted and combined themselves into a civil body for God's glory. It created a trust-filled basis for the ultimate societal experiment.

Their new world society endured a difficult time as winter approached the following year. Yet, they remained faithful. In the midst of a severe drought that threatened to destroy their harvest, the pilgrims prayed and fasted. In response to their faithfulness, the Lord brought crop-saving rain. Indeed, the pilgrims had much for which to be thankful as they established a feast that we now celebrate as Thanksgiving.

Their faithfulness and thankfulness provided witnessing opportunities to the American natives who observed the pilgrims and their relationship with the Lord. Because of their strong testimony of trust in Him, a native remarked:

> *Now I see that the Englishman's God is a good God; for he hath heard you, and sent you rain, and that without such tempest and thunder as we used to have with our rain; which after our Powawing [Indian worship] for it, breaks down the corn; whereas your corn stands whole and good still; surely, your God is a good God.*

He was a good God then, and He is today! And it is a light that we must not allow to dim.

LEAVING THEIR WARM NESTS

Several hundred miles south a few years before the pilgrim landing, the London Company established James Fort, also known as Jamestown, as the first permanent settlement in the New World. A rotation of guards was a necessary feature of the outpost, and their vigilance was required for the safety and security of the population. At each changing of the guard, they recited the following prayer:

> *We know, O Lord, we have the devil and all the gates of Hell against us, but if Thou O Lord be on our side, we care not who be against us. And seeing by Thy motion and work in our hearts, we have left our warm nests at home, and put our lives into Thy hands, principally to honor Thy name and advance the Kingdom of Thy Son, Lord give us leave to commit our lives into Thy hands, Amen.*

These guards were wise to acknowledge the pressing and pervasive threat of the devil and the gates of Hell. Yet, they were astute in relying on the protection of the Lord whose presence would be the deciding factor in their success or failure. They had bravely and faithfully left the safety of home to put their lives into His hands, to honor His name, and to advance the Kingdom of Christ. Their trust in Him provided a glimmer of hope for their fledgling society.

A SHINING CITY ON A HILL

American Historian Gordon S. Wood stated the following powerful truth about the core of our great nation:

> *The Revolution is the most important event in our history. It not only legally created the United States, but it infused into our culture the noblest ideals and highest aspirations, our beliefs in liberty, equality, and the happiness of ordinary people. Since there is no American ethnicity, these ideals and values are the only thing holding us together as a nation.*

The revolution didn't just begin in 1775 though. It began in those years shortly after the landing of the pilgrims, stemming from a common identity of trust in the Lord.

At his farewell speech on January 11, 1989, President Reagan shared the following:

> *I've spoken of the shining city all my political life, but I don't know if I ever quite communicated what I saw when I said it. But in my mind it was a tall, proud city built on rocks stronger than oceans, wind-swept, God-blessed, and teeming with people of all kinds living in harmony and peace; a city with free ports that hummed with commerce and creativity. And if there had to be city walls, the walls had doors and the doors were open to anyone with the will and the heart to get here. That's how I saw it, and see it still.*

Reagan's words hearken back to some poignant thoughts penned several centuries prior. Governor John Winthrop led the Massachusetts Bay Colony in the Seventeenth Century. In 1630, Winthrop wrote the following:

> *For we must consider that we shall be as a City upon a hill. The eyes of all people are upon us. So that if we shall deal falsely with our God in this work we have undertaken, and so cause him to withdraw his present help from us, we shall be made a story and a byword throughout the world.*

Our nation was designed to be a shining city on a hill. It was created to be the model for all of humanity. Yet, it could never hope to survive if it diverged from a trust in the Divine. And as Governor Winthrop warned, once we severed our society from trust in God, we would become a byword through the world – a cautionary tale for the rest of human history. Yet, if we would trust in God, we would provide a bright beacon of hope for all of humanity.

A DIVINE ORIGIN AND SANCTION

Nearly a century ago, Dr. Alice Baldwin published a study entitled *The New England Clergy and the American Revolution*. As a history professor at Duke University, Dr. Baldwin carefully mapped the concepts in our founding documents to Biblical concepts preached from American's pulpits long before the Revolution. Her findings are compelling:

> *The New England clergy preserved, extended, and popularized the essential doctrines of political philosophy, thus making familiar to every church-going New Englander long before 1763 not only the doctrines of natural right, the social contract, and the right of resistance but also the fundamental principle of American constitutional law, that government, like its citizens, is bound by law and when it transcends its authority it acts illegally.*

These and like sermons and pamphlets show clearly the continuity and strength of these political principles, how intimately they were associated with the Bible, which was interpreted to give them a divine origin and sanction, how the phrases, through long repetition and association with religion, were bitten deep into men's minds long before the outbreak of trouble with England.

Dr. Baldwin continues: "There is not a right asserted in the Declaration of Independence which had not been discussed by the New England clergy before 1763."

While governmental overreach accompanying the end of the French and Indian War in 1763 created the first spark of resentment between the colonists and the British government, the Biblical concepts that would guide the next few decades were already familiar to the Christian population. In fact, every element of the Declaration of Independence derived from a Biblical basis that had been preached from America's pulpits. Through their faith, the population understood that their human rights enjoyed Divine origin and sanction. And when they eventually heard the following from the Declaration, they knew where it all originated:

When in the course of human events, it becomes necessary for one people to dissolve the political bands which have connected them with another, and to assume among the powers of the earth, the separate and equal station to which the Laws of Nature and of Nature's God entitle them, a decent respect to the opinions of mankind requires that they should declare the causes which impel them to the separation.

THE SPARK OF A REVOLUTION

Cognizant of their natural God-given rights and filled with consternation about growing monarchical tyranny, the First Continental Congress began its two-month meeting on September 5, 1774. The members assembled there immediately recognized that they needed prayer to accomplish their important task. As the day opened on the morning of September 7, Jacob Duché prayed the following:

> *O Lord our Heavenly Father, high and mighty King of kings, and Lord of lords, who dost from thy throne behold all the dwellers on earth and reignest with power supreme and uncontrolled over all the Kingdoms, Empires and Governments; look down in mercy, we beseech Thee, on these our American States, who have fled to Thee from the rod of the oppressor and thrown themselves on Thy gracious protection, desiring to be henceforth dependent only on Thee. To Thee have they appealed for the righteousness of their cause; to Thee do they now look up for that countenance and support, which Thou alone canst give. Take them, therefore, Heavenly Father, under Thy nurturing care; give them wisdom in Council and valor in the field; defeat the malicious designs of our cruel adversaries; convince them of the unrighteousness of their Cause and if they persist in their sanguinary purposes, of own unerring justice, sounding in their hearts, constrain them to drop the weapons of war from their unnerved hands in the day of battle!*
>
> *Be Thou present, O God of wisdom, and direct the councils of this honorable assembly; enable them to settle things on the best and surest foundation. That the scene of blood may be speedily closed; that order, harmony and peace may be effectually restored, and truth and justice, religion and piety, prevail and flourish amongst the people. Preserve the health of their bodies and vigor of their minds; shower down on them and the millions they here represent, such temporal blessings as Thou seest expedient for them in this world and crown them with everlasting glory in the world to come. All this we ask in the name and through the merits of Jesus Christ, Thy Son and our Savior.*

The leaders of our first governing body humbly recognized the need for prayer as they went about their deliberations. They prayed for personal and national protection. They prayed for direction and wisdom. They prayed for their own physical and mental well-being. They prayed for their weighty responsibility representing millions of colonial citizens. They prayed to be dependent only on God because they trusted in Him!

In addition to Duché's prayer on September 7, 1774, the First Continental Congress spent time reading Psalm 35. John Adams wrote the following to his wife Abigail about the impact of prayer and Bible reading as the First Continental Congress began its important role in colonial governance: "I never saw a greater Effect upon an Audience. It seemed as if Heaven had ordained that Psalm to be read on that Morning." Regarding the time of prayer and Bible reading, he went on to write: "it has had an excellent Effect upon every Body here." Faith, belief, and connectivity to God created resolve. It was a trust-fueled start to something that would be magnified in the looming conflict to follow.

A CHURCH LAWN IN LEXINGTON

On March 22, 1775, Connecticut's Governor Jonathan Trumball proclaimed April 19 of that year as a day of prayer and fasting. His calling included the following:

> *God would graciously pour out His Holy Spirit on us to bring us to a thorough repentance and effectual reformation that our iniquities may not be our ruin; that He would restore, preserve and secure the liberties of this and all the other British American colonies, and make the land a mountain of Holiness, and habitation of righteousness forever.*

A month prior to its first shot, Massachusetts' neighbor had committed to pray for liberty on the very day that the Revolutionary began. They prayed for a pouring out of God's Spirit. They prayed for repentance. They prayed for reformation. They prayed for restoration and preservation.

They prayed that this would be a land of holiness and righteousness forever.

The first shots of the Revolutionary War were fired by the British on a church lawn in Lexington, Massachusetts on April 19, 1775. The Massachusetts Militia faced down 700 British regulars who were enroute to capture supplies and weapons at Concord.

Deacon John Parker boldly led the men to stand their ground under the encouragement of Reverend Jonas Clark whose church lay abeam this first revolutionary battleground. Indeed, these Christian patriots did so boldly: "consistent with a determined resolution and Christian firmness, in defence of their rights and liberties which they held dearer than life." After the confrontation in Lexington on that day, eight colonial men lay dead and ten wounded after the unprovoked British volley of fire. After years of sermons on citizenship and God-given-rights, these patriots fought and died under the shadow of the house of God.

Reverend Clark went on to say:

> But it is not by us alone that this day is to be noticed. The ever memorable day is full of importance to all around, to this whole land and nation; and big with the fate of Great Britain and America. For this remarkable day will an important era begin for both America and Britain. And from the nineteenth of April, 1775, we may venture to predict, will be dated in future history THE LIBERTY or SLAVERY of the AMERICAN WORLD, according as a sovereign God shall see fit to smile or frown upon the interesting cause in which we are engaged.

Ralph Waldo Emerson's Concord Hymn echoed these sentiments, declaring the skirmish as "the shot heard round the world."

From its beginnings, men and women of faith have had a substantial impact on this nation. Through trust and faith in the Lord, they stood fast without wavering.

PUNCTUAL ATTENDANCE

On June 15, 1775, General George Washington was appointed Commander in Chief of the Continental Army, taking command two and a half weeks later. On July 4, 1775, exactly a year before the Second Continental Congress proclaimed colonial independence and more than two months after the first shots of the Revolutionary War, General Washington published the following admonition to the soldiers under his command:

> *The General most earnestly requires, and expects, a due observance of those articles of war, established for the Government of the army, which forbid profane cursing, swearing and drunkenness; And in like manner requires and expects, of all Officers, and Soldiers, not engaged on actual duty, a punctual attendance on divine Service, to implore the blessings of heaven upon the means used for our safety and defence.*

Washington's General Orders contained the short but critical components of proper behavior and right living. The men were to live in a way that was worthy of their unit, their army, and their cause. He required them to personify their common dream. If they were to be followed, then they must BE something worth following. Elsewhere in the Orders, General Washington required officers to properly care for their men. And yes, General Washington ordered his men to attend church, worship and pray.

The officers and soldiers of the Continental Army were to be worthy examples. They were to be clean and humble. They were to be upright and bold. They were to be faithful and prayerful. They were to trust in God!

THE KING OF AMERICA

As General Washington was leading his men in their important task, others were preparing the populace for a surge toward independence.

On January 10, 1776, Thomas Paine published a landmark document that fanned the flames of independence in colonial America. A brilliantly written pamphlet, Common Sense swept through the colonies as a well-reasoned rationale for separation from the British Empire. In his own words, Paine described his endeavor in the following way: "In the following pages I offer nothing more than simple facts, plain arguments, and common sense." Paine's arguments were infused with Biblical literacy and familiarity.

After describing the purpose of government, uplifting the importance of uniqueness, explaining the pitfalls of monarchy, and expounding upon the blessings of God, Thomas Paine proclaimed that there was only one natural conclusion:

> *But where say some is the King of America? I'll tell you Friend, he reigns above, and doth not make havoc of mankind like the Royal Brute of Britain. Yet that we may not appear to be defective even in earthly honors, let a day be solemnly set apart for proclaiming the charter; let it be brought forth placed on the divine law, the word of God; let a crown be placed thereon, by which the world may know, that so far as we approve of monarchy, that in America THE LAW IS KING. For as in absolute governments the King is law, so in free countries the law ought to be King; and there ought to be no other. But lest any ill use should afterwards arise, let the crown at the conclusion of the ceremony be demolished, and scattered among the people whose right it is.*

According to Paine, a figure often equated with secularism, God was to be King of America with his crowned Word as the nation's foundation. According to this sage Founder, there was to be no other.

A public that trusted in God was now ready for a surge towards independence.

CHAPTER 5

THE SPARK THAT IGNITED A MOVEMENT OF TRUST

BY JOHN TEICHERT

San Diego, California has one of the world's most spectacular Fourth of July firework shows. Fireworks are launched from four locations, entertaining a crowd of over a half a million expectant fans for nearly 20 minutes … usually. On July 4th, 2012, things didn't go as expected. Due to a computer malfunction, all the fireworks from all the locations went off simultaneously. In less than 30 spectacular seconds, the show was over. It didn't last as expected.

Our Founders designed this nation to last. They walked in Him. They rooted this nation in Him and built it up in Him. They stablished it in faith. They trusted in Him.

In our founding document, the Declaration of Independence, the fingerprints of our God and their faith are evident and abundant:

- God entitles us to our rights – "to which the Laws of nature and Nature's God entitle [us]" (Romans 13:1)

- We are created and created equal – "We hold these truths to be self-evident, that all men are created equal" (Genesis 1:27)

- We all share the same source of liberty – we are "endowed by [our] Creator with certain unalienable Rights" (Galatians 5:1)

- Governments are to be designed to secure our God-given rights – "that to secure these rights, Governments are instituted among Men" (II Corinthians 3:17)

- God is the Supreme Judge – "appealing to the Supreme Judge of the world for the rectitude of our intentions" (II Samuel 2:10)

- God is powerful and trustworthy – "with a firm reliance on the protection of divine Providence" (I Peter 5:6-7)

This nation has lasted because of its roots: "As ye have therefore received Christ Jesus the Lord, so walk ye in him: Rooted and built up in him, and stablished in the faith, as ye have been taught, abounding therein with thanksgiving" (Colossians 2:6-7).

On our nation's 61st Birthday, John Quincy Adams boldly proclaimed the following to the people of Newburyport, Massachusetts:

> *Is it not that, in the chain of human events, the birthday of the nation is indissolubly linked with the birthday of the Savior? That it forms a leading event in the progress of the gospel dispensation? Is it not that the Declaration of Independence first organized the social compact on the foundation of the Redeemer's mission upon earth? That it laid the corner stone of human government upon the first precepts of Christianity, and gave to the world the first irrevocable pledge of the fulfillment of the prophecies, announced directly from Heaven at the birth of the Savior and predicted by the greatest of the Hebrew prophets six hundred years before?*

Though we know the United States of America does not fulfill the prophecies of the Old Testament, our nation is fundamentally tied to Christianity, and our nation's birth is indissolubly linked to the birthday of our Saviour. Our cornerstone of human government, the Declaration of Independence, is laid upon the first precepts of Christianity. Our founding document is a social compact that is an intentional extension of the Redeemer's mission. Thus, Independence Day is a time to rightfully celebrate the truths of Christmas Day. The fireworks of the Fourth of July illuminate the powerful truth that Christ's birth and our trust in Him is inscribed on our national character.

APPEALING TO THE SUPREME JUDGE

On April 12, 1776, the Fourth Provincial Congress of North Carolina adopted a resolution now known as the Halifax Resolves. In doing so, the 83 members of this body unanimously approved the first official call for American independence. North Carolinian delegates were now officially empowered to vote for separation from Great Britain at the Continental Congress.

Talking about independence was one thing; approving a resolution that promoted independence was something far greater. Believing that they could achieve separation was one thing; taking active steps towards separation was something far greater. Bemoaning grievances against the British was one thing; signing one's name to a list of grievances against the British was something far greater. The Fourth Provincial Congress of North Carolina turned their faith into trusting activity. Otherwise, the cause of independence in this land would have died before it began.

On June 7, 1776, Richard Henry Lee of Virginia proposed the following to the Continental Congress:

> *Resolved, That these United Colonies are, and of right ought to be, free and independent States, that they are absolved from all allegiance to the British Crown, and that all political connection between them and the State of Great Britain, is, and ought to be, totally dissolved. That it is expedient forthwith to take the most effectual measures for forming foreign Alliances. That a plan of confederation be prepared and transmitted to the respective Colonies for their consideration and approbation.*

These words formed the basis for the Declaration of Independence a month later. In that latter document, the Founders (in one long sentence) closely paralleled Lee's thoughts:

We, therefore, the Representatives of the united States of America, in General Congress, Assembled, appealing to the Supreme Judge of the world for the rectitude of our intentions, do, in the Name, and by the Authority of the good People of these Colonies, solemnly publish and declare, That these United Colonies are, and of Right ought to be Free and Independent States; that they are Absolved from all Allegiance to the British Crown, and that all political connection between them and the State of Great Britain, is and ought to be totally dissolved; and that as Free and Independent States, they have full Power to levy War, conclude Peace, contract Alliances, establish Commerce, and to do all other Acts and Things which Independent States may of right do.

Our Founders turned to the one and only Ultimate Authority who was imminently trustworthy. They didn't appeal to other nations. They didn't appeal to foreign military powers. They didn't appeal to their own reason, education, or philosophy. They didn't appeal to the prevailing cultural morality. Instead, they appealed to God, thus turning to the Supreme Judge of the world. It was to Him that they sought adjudication of their righteous intent – the rectitude of their intentions.

FIRM RELIANCE

The last line of the Declaration of Independence humbles me every time I read it:

> *And for the support of this Declaration, with a firm reliance on the protection of divine Providence, we mutually pledge to each other our Lives, our Fortunes and our sacred Honor.*

These were educated, experienced, courageous, and competent men. They had wisdom, might, and riches. Yet, they firmly relied upon one thing as they signed that glorious revolutionary document that would be seen as a public declaration of treason in the eyes of British authorities.

These great men of our founding recognized that they were not sufficient to the task of forming a new nation. Their strength was not sufficient. Their wisdom was not sufficient. Their courage was not sufficient. Their military might was not sufficient. Their economic resources were not sufficient. Their leadership abilities were not sufficient.

They recognized that they alone could not carry the weight of Christian citizenship. They also recognized that they need not try to do so as they staked their lives, their fortunes, and their reputations on the concepts contained in that formative and foundational document.

Instead, they trusted in God and firmly relied upon Him. They rested in His protection for their support. They recognized one important truth that would elude any culture that breeds and promotes self-sufficiency – that their sufficiency was of God. This last line buoyed everything that came before it, conveying an illuminating trust in God that would light the difficult path ahead.

THIRTY-FIVE WORDS THAT CHANGED THE WORLD

One 35-word sentence stands out above all others in the Declaration. It may be the most profound sentence ever penned by human hand and conceived of by human mind:

> *We hold these truths to be self-evident, that all men are created equal, that they are endowed by their Creator with certain unalienable Rights, that among these are Life, Liberty and the pursuit of Happiness.*

While an entire book could be written on the spiritual and practical significance of such a concept, a few thoughts will suffice here.

It starts with an understanding of an essential truth that we are CREATED.

We are not an accident! We have not been formed by odds-defeating cosmic chance. We are not amoral creatures void of purpose because we are unformed and unremarkable. We are not the result of a preposterous process of vectorless mutations, ruthless selections, and soulless instincts.

Instead, we have been carefully created by a loving, all-knowing, purpose-providing God. We are fearfully and wonderfully made, carefully knit together as preborn babies. The Creator has formed and fashioned each one of us. As a result, our lives have inherent structure, purpose, meaning, value, and worth.

While this profound sentence in the Declaration of Independence reminds us that we were CREATED, it also continues by acknowledging that God's plan is far better than even that. We are created EQUAL! We have been crafted and formed by our Glorious Maker in the image of God Himself.

None of this means that we are cookie-cutter, assembly-line-formed robotic outputs of creation. Such equity would mandate a mundane milieu for humanity. Instead, we have been formed in equality. Yet, all of us amazingly have our own courses, walk our own paths, embody a diversity of gifts, and yield complementary elements of impact.

All the while we can rest in the all-consuming truth of God's love. The same God worketh in each of us. He has provided us a faith to follow in our own contexts and circumstances. He has also yielded His Son for salvation and His Spirit for steadfastness. Finally, he punctuates His stunning plan of equality with a exclamation point of supernatural undeserved equity for those who trust in Him – an eternity in heaven through the shed blood of His Son.

This single 35-word sentence gets even better than that, particularly when amplified by the ones that came before and the one that follows. Our Founders recognized that God Himself is the source of all human rights and liberties. Specifically, man is given rights and liberties "to which the Laws of Nature and of Nature's God entitle them." To these humble men it was self-evident that man is "endowed by their Creator with certain unalienable Rights."

According to our Founders, then, what was the role of government? Our Declaration of Independence makes this role clear: "That to secure these rights, Governments are instituted among Men deriving their just powers from the consent of the governed."

Make no mistake, the role of government is to preserve rights given to us by God. Government is never to be the source of rights, only the securer of rights. Any governmental power is to be ordained by a trustworthy God and consented to by man. As engraved on the walls of the Jefferson Memorial: "God who gave us life gave us liberty. Can the liberties of a nation be secure when we have removed a conviction that these liberties are the gift of God?"

God gave us life, he gave us liberty, and he gave us the opportunity to pursue happiness. We must never rob the Lord of the appreciation fully due to Him for these blessings in our lives. Once we lose sight of the source of these rights, we quickly drift away from liberty and towards bondage.

Rabbi Sacks, the Chief Rabbi of the United Hebrew Congregations of the British Commonwealth from 1991 to 2013 reminds us that America's "source of inspiration was the Hebrew Bible." He goes on to say that "the tree of liberty has religious roots. Don't believe you can sever these roots and have the tree of liberty survive." Trusting in God is fundamentally interwoven into His plan for our highest human aspirations.

John Adams immediately understood the importance of our nation's declaration of independence, both the act and the document itself. It was on July 2, 1776 that the Continental Congress approved the following resolution: "That these United Colonies are, and of right ought to be, free and independent States, that they are absolved from all allegiance to the British Crown, and that all political connection between them and the State of Great Britain is, and ought to be, totally dissolved." The public declaration of these sentiments occurred two days later, memorialized in our Declaration of Independence.

John Adams wrote to Abigail describing his thoughts about the excitement of such a remarkable step of boldness:

> *(This) will be the most memorable Epocha, in the history*
> *of America. I am apt to believe that it will be celebrated, by*

> *succeeding Generations, as the great anniversary Festival.*
> *It ought to be commemorated, as the Day of Deliverance*
> *by solemn Acts of Devotion to God Almighty. It ought*
> *to be solemnized with Pomp and Parade with Shows,*
> *Games, Sports, Guns, Bells, Bonfires and Illuminations*
> *from one End of this Continent to the other from this*
> *Time forward forever more.*

Fireworks, fanfare, and faith-filled fellowship were foreseen as an outpouring of astonishment of this most memorable Epocha in the history of America. This celebration was meant to last much longer than the 15-second firework show in San Diego in 2012.

It was meant to endure!

CHAPTER 6

AT ALL TIMES NECESSARY

BY JOHN TEICHERT

On July 9, 1776, General George Washington ordered that the newly signed Declaration of Independence be read to the American Continental Army. On that evening on their parade grounds in New York City with the British Army closing in on them, 30,000 American soldiers heard those words proclaiming liberty and announcing separation from tyranny.

General Washington's rationale for doing so was clearly described in his General Order from that day:

> *The General hopes this important Event will serve as a fresh incentive to every officer, and soldier, to act with Fidelity and Courage, as knowing that now the peace and safety of his Country depends (under God) solely on the success of our arms: And that he is now in the service of a State, possessed of sufficient power to reward his merit, and advance him to the highest Honors of a free Country.*

This proclamation had its intended impact. On that same evening, a large statue of King George III was torn down in New York City and melted into bullets to add to the revolutionary arsenal. Though it was several years before victory was ultimately achieved, the spark of freedom that was lit on that evening caused the sacred fires of liberty to burn within the hearts of every soldier.

In that same General Order, General Washington ordered the following:

> *The Honorable Continental Congress having been pleased to allow a Chaplain to each Regiment, with the pay of Thirty-three Dollars and one third per month— The Colonels or commanding officers of each regiment are directed to procure Chaplains accordingly; persons of good Characters and exemplary lives – To see that all inferior officers and soldiers pay them a suitable respect and attend carefully upon religious exercises: The blessing and protection of Heaven are at all times necessary but especially so in times of public distress and danger—The General hopes and trusts, that every officer, and man, will endeavour so to live, and act, as becomes a Christian Soldier defending the dearest Rights and Liberties of his country.*

General Washington knew that God must be involved if the American revolutionary cause was going to be successful.

INCLINING THEIR HEARTS TO GOD

At the end of August 1776, the Continental Army faced their first major battle after the Declaration of Independence. In what is known as the Battle of Long Island, the Battle of Brooklyn, or the Battle of Brooklyn Heights the Americans found themselves surrounded with their backs to the East River. Hour-by-hour, British troops crept closer to the Continental front lines. The only way to retain the hope for independence was to preserve the Continental Army and escape by boat.

One of General Washington's challenges during the retreat was to escape silently while convincing the British that the Continental Army was still arrayed at their defensive positions during the night. The Continental Army tricked the British by carefully choreographing shots and heavily utilizing campfires. The ruse worked, and the British Army didn't suspect that the façade was anything other than reality. Undoubtedly, God had helped the Continental Army in this respect, clouding the judgment of the battle-hardened British force and taking a battleplan from ancient Israel:

"For the Lord had made the host of the Syrians to hear a noise of chariots, and a noise of horses, even the noise of a great host: and they said one to another, Lo, the king of Israel hath hired against us the kings of the Hittites, and the kings of the Egyptians, to come upon us" (II Kings 7:6).

General Washington arranged a brilliant retreat plan during the perilous night of August 29. It required silence, coordination, and deception. It also required heavenly intervention.

At daybreak on August 30, the retreat was incomplete. As the sun arose, a thick and unexpected fog sprung up and concealed the remaining maneuver, providing the few necessary hours to allow all men and supplies to be out of British range before clearing. During that night, 9,000 men escaped – the Lord had saved them. Washington recognized the truth from his General Order: "the blessing and protection of Heaven are at all times necessary but especially so in times of public distress and danger."

And the ability to survive to fight again was the best that Washington's Army could hope for in their first few years of the Revolution, and they trusted in God for their ability to do so. Yet, as the year ended, they had a small chance to strike back.

At daybreak on December 26, 1776, General Washington led the Continental Army on a bold surprise attack of Trenton, New Jersey. After a Christmas night crossing of the icy Delaware River, the Revolutionary Army successful struck the British stronghold with almost no losses. It was described by Yale President Ezra Stiles as a "heaven inspired" move to break the trend of defeats. The strategic impact of this battle was massive. The ability of the young nation to continue its pursuit of independence was "sealed and confirmed by God Almighty in the victory of General Washington at Trenton."

A few days later, the continuity of the Revolutionary Army was at stake. As the New Year approached at the end of 1776, the hopes of the Continental Army were indeed bleak. For much of the year, they had been on the losing end of their battles, and the enemy seemed to have the upper hand in all respects. To compound their problems, the revolutionary forces were out-gunned and out-resourced. As winter closed in on them, they were low on supplies, equipment, and uniforms. Though they had recently won the Christmastime victory at Trenton that could have boosted morale, the entire army was afforded the opportunity to permanently leave their spots on the battlefront when the terms of their enlistment ended as the calendar turned to 1777. The only hope of an independent America was for men to step forward and volunteer to remain in the battle. In the waning hours of 1776, General Washington addressed his troops with the following words:

> *My brave fellows, you have done all I asked you to do, and more than could be reasonably expected, but your country is at stake, your wives, your houses, and all that you hold dear. You have worn yourselves out with fatigues and hardships, but we know not how to spare you. If you will consent to stay one month longer, you will render that service to the cause of liberty, and to your country, which you can probably never do under any other circumstance.*

Nathanael Greene wrote about the men's response: "God Almighty inclined their hearts to listen to the proposal and they engaged anew." One-by-one, men stepped forward to renew their commitment to the cause and reaffirm their dedication through reenlistment. It was a miracle for a fledgling nation that trusted in the Lord. American historian David McCullough said the following about that pivotal year:

> *The year 1776, celebrated as the birth year of the nation and for the signing of the Declaration of Independence, was for those who carried the fight for independence forward a year of all-too-few victories, or sustained suffering, disease, hunger, desertion, cowardice, disillusionment, defeat, terrible discouragement, and fear, and they would never forget, but also of phenomenal*

courage and bedrock devotion to country, and that, too, they would never forget.

Especially for those who had been with Washington and who knew what a close call it was at the beginning – how often circumstance, storms, contrary winds, the oddities or strengths of individual character had made the difference – the outcome seemed little short of a miracle.

AN INDISPENSABLE DUTY OF ALL MEN

The following year didn't fare much better for the revolutionary cause, yet under God they survived. As the year came to an end, Dr. Benjamin Rush recalls a conversation with his friend John Adams:

Upon my return from the army to Baltimore in the winter of 1777, I sat next to John Adams in Congress, and upon my whispering to him and asking him if he thought we should succeed in our struggle with Great Britain, he answered me, "Yes – if we fear God and repent of our sins."

Success hinged on their trust in God, and they rightfully and practically demonstrated their thankfulness to Him.

The 1777 Thanksgiving Proclamation by the Continental Congress was bursting with thankfulness, praise, and gratitude. The colonists recognized that it was their indispensable duty to uplift the Lord's name in this way. Yet, in historical context it was not a time that thankfulness, praise, and gratitude came naturally.

The Continental Army was years from victory. In fact, the British had just captured Philadelphia, and the poorly fed and equipped revolutionaries were about ready to settle down at Valley Forge for a harsh winter a short distance from the British ranks. The Americans had no major allies and were struggling to maintain themselves as a viable fighting force. Yet, they took time to express gratitude. The totality of this proclamation is worthy of a full read.

FORASMUCH as it is the indispensable Duty of all Men to adore the superintending Providence of Almighty God; to acknowledge with Gratitude their Obligation to him for Benefits received, and to implore such farther Blessings as they stand in Need of: And it having pleased him in his abundant Mercy, not only to continue to us the innumerable Bounties of his common Providence; but also to smile upon us in the Prosecution of a just and necessary War, for the Defense and Establishment of our unalienable Rights and Liberties; particularly in that he hath been pleased, in so great a Measure, to prosper the Means used for the Support of our Troops, and to crown our Arms with most signal success:

It is therefore recommended to the legislative or executive Powers of these UNITED STATES to set apart THURSDAY, the eighteenth Day of December next, for SOLEMN THANKSGIVING and PRAISE: That at one Time and with one Voice, the good People may express the grateful Feelings of their Hearts, and consecrate themselves to the Service of their Divine Benefactor; and that, together with their sincere Acknowledgments and Offerings, they may join the penitent Confession of their manifold Sins, whereby they had forfeited every Favor; and their humble and earnest Supplication that it may please GOD through the Merits of JESUS CHRIST, mercifully to forgive and blot them out of Remembrance; That it may please him graciously to afford his Blessing on the Governments of these States respectively, and prosper the public Council of the whole: To inspire our Commanders, both by Land and Sea, and all under them, with that Wisdom and Fortitude which may render them fit Instruments, under the Providence of Almighty GOD, to secure for these United States, the greatest of all human Blessings, INDEPENDENCE and PEACE: That it may please him, to prosper the Trade and Manufactures of the People, and the Labor of the Husbandman, that our Land may yield its Increase: To take Schools and Seminaries of Education, so necessary for cultivating the Principles of true Liberty, Virtue and Piety, under his nurturing Hand; and to prosper the Means of Religion, for the promotion and enlargement of that Kingdom, which consisteth 'in Righteousness, Peace and Joy in the Holy Ghost.'

And it is further recommended, That servile Labor, and such Recreation, as, though at other Times innocent, may be unbecoming the Purpose of this Appointment, be omitted on so solemn an Occasion.

It is with this spirit of gratitude, humility, and trust, that Washington's Army encamped at Valley Forge.

SUBLIME HEROISM

The days, the weeks, and the months at Valley Forge tested the endurance of the American Continental Army. General Washington wrote the following about their conditions, their constitution, and their character:

For without arrogance or the smallest deviation from truth it may be said, that no history now extant can furnish an instance of an army's suffering such uncommon hardships as ours has done, and bearing them with the same patience and fortitude. To see men, without clothes to cover their nakedness, without blankets to lay on, without shoes, by which their marches might be traced by blood from their feet, and almost as often without provisions as with them, marching through frost and snow, and at Christmas taking up their Winter Quarters within a day's march of the enemy, without a house or hut to cover them till they could be built, and submitting to it without a murmur, is a mark of patience and obedience which in my opinion can scarce be paralleled.

So how did they survive such conditions? They trusted in God and prayed. In President Ronald Reagan's 1986 Thanksgiving Proclamation, he stated the following about General Washington:

> *One of the most inspiring portrayals of American history is that of George Washington on his knees in the snow at Valley Forge. That moving image personifies and testifies to our Founders' dependence upon Divine Providence during the darkest hours of our Revolutionary struggle. It was then - when our mettle as a Nation was tested most severely - that the Sovereign and Judge of nations heard our plea and came to our assistance in the form of aid from France. Thereupon General Washington immediately called for a special day of thanksgiving among his troops.*

In light of the severe difficulties the men faced at Valley Forge, General Washington turned to the one thing that he knew could make a difference – he prayed. The image of Washington kneeling in prayer has been described as the most sublime in American history. A Quaker named Isaac Potts described the prayer of Washington in this way: "Such a prayer I never heard from the lips of man." His conclusion after seeing the fervent prayer of this founding father: "it was the cause of God and America could prevail." Witnessing one man's trusting and fervent prayer convinced a skeptic that victory was possible.

General Washington turned to God in time of crisis at Valley Forge because he had an established relationship with Him. Throughout his life, he recognized that it was not enough to depend on his own courage and goodness, but that he needed help from his Father and preserver. It wasn't enough to ask for protection in time of crisis, but the Lord was needed in his day-to-day life to abide by the standards of right and wrong. Washington's sufficiency was of God and not of himself. That transcendent picture of Washington praying personifies this important truth. But Washington also called for others to join him in trusting dependence on the Lord.

General Washington published a set of General Orders on the first day of the Revolutionary Army's time at Valley Forge – December 17, 1777. It included the following charge to his men:

> *Tomorrow being the day set apart by the Honorable Congress for public Thanksgiving and Praise; and duty calling us devoutly to express our grateful acknowledgements to God for the manifold blessings he has granted us—The General directs that the army remain in its present quarters, and that the Chaplains perform divine service with their several Corps and brigades—And earnestly exhorts, all officers and soldiers, whose absence is not indispensably necessary, to attend with reverence the solemnities of the day.*

These men were busy as they started their time of winter lodging at Valley Forge. They lacked food; they lacked clothing; they lacked equipment. They needed to train, to drill, to exercise, and to march. They lacked shelter from the harsh elements and desperately needed to build structures to protect themselves from the brutal conditions.

Yet, they prioritized a time of worship. They uplifted a period of grateful acknowledgement to God for the manifold blessing He had granted them. More than clothes, shelter, food, and training, they needed to make an investment in trusting faithfulness. They needed to attend with reverence the solemnities of the day. It set the stage for sustained and necessary resilience.

The conditions for the American Continental Army were brutal during that winter. That military force was under-equipped, under-fed, and under clothed. Of the 12,000 soldiers that entered camp in December of 1777, over 2,000 died before they left in the spring of 1778.

Yet, the American Continental Army recognized the importance of these cold, harsh, long months. Through their patience and fortitude, they saw an opportunity to ready themselves for the battles to come.

Up to that point, the main army of the Americans had yet to see success against the British in force-on-force conflict. Yes, the revolutionaries had seen some victories during small scale skirmishes during the war that had already lasted over 2½ years. They had been successful at places like Concord, Dorchester Heights, Brooklyn, Trenton, and Princeton; however, they had not seen any signs of success that would indicate that they were headed for true victory.

Thus, during that long winter they trained. They exercised. They drilled. They were determined to create a disciplined, professional force that would be ready for whatever they would see in the battles to come. They readied themselves for all contingencies instead of spending the time sulking about their miserable conditions.

Shortly after they left Valley Forge in 1778, they faced their first test in a main force-on-force engagement called the Battle of Monmouth. Their readiness was put to the test, and for the first time, it was the British who disengaged from the battle. The American Continental Army prevailed, proving that they could face down a trained and professional British force. It wasn't a huge victory on its own, but it signaled hope for the entire revolutionary cause. And it was all based on trusting prayerfulness and a desperate dependence upon God.

In his biography on George Washington, Benson Lossing wrote the following:

> *For in all the world's history, we have no record of purer devotion, holier sincerity, or more pious self-sacrifice, than was there exhibited in the camp of Washington. The courage of the battlefield dwindles almost into insignificance when compared with that sublime heroism displayed by the American soldiery at Valley Forge, in the midst of frost and snow, disease and destitution.*

ALL OTHER DEPENDENCES FAIL US

The war raged on for several more years, but the period following Valley Forge started to see victories for the American cause. Their trust in the Lord remained the lynchpin of their success and a core of their character. Throughout, General Washington maintained his reliance on the Lord's intervention and eyewitness of God's power throughout the Revolutionary War. In 1781, he wrote, "We have, as you very justly observe, abundant reason to thank Providence for its many favorable interpositions in our behalf. It has at times been my only dependence, for all other resources seemed to have failed us."

It is difficult to ignore the Lord's mighty influence on America's victory in the Revolutionary War from beginning to end that allowed victory over the well-trained and resourced British force. The uncharacteristic weather that protected the early colonist force positioned precariously on the Dorchester Heights shattered the image of British invulnerability. The thick fog that secured a retreat of Washington's army kept the colonist forces intact after the Battle of New York. The early hard frost that prompted General Howe to halt his forces in Trenton for the winter gave the beleaguered colonist army a much-needed respite in a secure sanctuary. Finally, the unexpected squall that halted the British escape from Yorktown secured the colonists' final victory.

Looking back on their revolutionary experience, President Washington wrote the following in 1789:

> *The man must be bad indeed who can look upon the events of the American Revolution without feeling the warmest gratitude towards the great Author of the Universe whose divine interposition was so frequently manifested in our behalf. And it is my earnest prayer that we may so conduct ourselves as to merit a continuance of those blessings with which we have hitherto been favored.*

CHAPTER 7

THE WORK OF A DIVINE PROVIDENCE

BY JOHN TEICHERT

In the midst of the Revolutionary War, the Second Continental Congress approved the Articles of Confederation on November 15, 1777. This document, our nation's first constitution, established the form of our federal government as we fought for and eventually won our independence. Yet, it was far from perfect.

By 1787, it had become clear that major structural changes were needed to create a viable and sustainable federal government. With this in mind, a Constitutional Convention met in Philadelphia at the Pennsylvania State House to revise the flawed construct. As they looked at the changes required, however, they realized that the only real way forward was to start over. In those hot summer months, from May 25 to September 17, those Founders created the United States Constitution. In 116 days, the world saw an innovation of government unmatched in human history. These men recognized the shortcomings of doing things the way they had always been done, refused to accept a few small fixes to cover up deep flaws, committed to doing something grand, and worked together despite their differences. They did it all through a profound trust in God.

Founding Father Benjamin Rush punctuated God's great hand in the results with the following poignant thought: "I do not believe that the Constitution was the offspring of inspiration, but I am as satisfied that it is as much the work of a Divine Providence as any of the miracles recorded in the Old and New Testament."

Sometimes, however, these great men needed a human nudge to return to their firm reliance on Him.

PROFOUND ADVICE FROM AN ELDER STATESMAN

As the end of June approached in 1787 and the temperatures rose in Philadelphia, so did the tempers at the Constitutional Convention. After several weeks of debate and deliberation, the men that were assembled there faced several impasses that threatened to derail the new nation before it even began. Recognizing the precariousness of the situation, elder statesman Dr. Benjamin Franklin rose to his feet to state the following:

> *In this situation of this Assembly, groping as it were in the dark to find political truth, and scarce able to distinguish it when presented to us, how has it happened, Sir, that we have not hitherto once thought of humbly applying to the Father of lights to illuminate our understandings? In the beginning of the Contest with Great Britain, when we were sensible of danger, we had daily prayer in this room for the divine protection. Our prayers, Sir, were heard, and they were graciously answered. All of us who were engaged in the struggle must have observed frequent instances of a superintending providence in our favor.*
>
> *To that kind providence we owe this happy opportunity of consulting in peace on the means of establishing our future national felicity. And have we now forgotten that powerful friend? Or do we imagine that we no longer need his assistance?*

Ben Franklin, a man not known for a religious fervency, recognized the fruitlessness of continuing on in the absence of daily prayer for our nation. What sense did it make to grope about in darkness when a light was readily available? What sense did it make for them to imagine that they no longer needed the Lord's assistance? What sense did it make to depart from the proven instances of superintending providence in their favor? Apart from a trust in God, the loose collection of states had no hope of joining into a viable nation. Apart from God, they were destined to stumble and fail.

Dr. Franklin went on to say:

> *I have lived, Sir, a long time, and the longer I live, the more convincing proofs I see of this truth – that God Governs in the affairs of men. And if a sparrow cannot fall to the ground without his notice, is it probable that an empire can rise without his aid? We have been assured, Sir, in the sacred writings, that "except the Lord build the House they labour in vain that build it." I firmly believe this; and I also believe that without his concurring aid we shall succeed in this political building no better, than the Builders of Babel: We shall be divided by our little partial local interests; our projects will be confounded, and we ourselves shall become a reproach and bye word down to future ages. And what is worse, mankind may hereafter from this unfortunate instance, despair of establishing Governments by Human wisdom and leave it to chance, war and conquest.*

> *I therefore beg leave to move – that henceforth prayers imploring the assistance of Heaven, and its blessings on our deliberations, be held in this Assembly every morning before we proceed to business, and that one or more of the Clergy of this City be requested to officiate in that Service."*

As Ben Franklin reminded them, whatever they attempted to build would be in vain unless they relinquished control unto the Lord. How did Dr. Franklin recommend that the Founding Fathers put this truth into action? His recommendation was a simple one, to pray daily for our nation while imploring the assistance of a trustworthy God. The results were finalized on September 17, 1787 because Franklin helped them remember their unique source of strength – firmly relying on the protection of Divine Providence.

Several steps were necessary before this Constitution could be ratified and the new government formed. The Bill of Rights was a key component of the final ratification process, and it begins with our first freedom.

OUR FIRST FREEDOM

On November 16, 1993, *The New York Times* reported the following about a new piece of legislation known as the Religious Freedom Restoration Act: "President Clinton today signed into law legislation requiring the Government to meet stringent standards before instituting measures that might interfere with religious practices."

About this law, President Clinton said the following:

> *The free exercise of religion has been called the first freedom, that which originally sparked the development of the full range of the Bill of Rights.*
>
> *What this law basically says is that the Government should be held to a very high level of proof before it interferes with someone's free exercise of religion. This judgment is shared by the people of the United States as well as by the Congress. We believe strongly that we can never, we can never be too vigilant in this work.*

The 1993 Religious Freedom Restoration Act passed with overwhelming majorities. The House Bill passed without a single objection, sponsored by Democrat Chuck Schumer and Republican Chris Cox. The Senate Bill passed by a vote of 97-3, sponsored by Democrat Ted Kennedy and Republican Orrin Hatch. Of the bipartisan nature of this effort, President Clinton commented: "I'm told that, as many of the people in the coalition worked together across ideological and religious lines, some new friendships were formed and some new trust was established, which shows, I suppose, that the power of God is such that even in the legislative process miracles can happen."

Society has changed drastically in the past three decades, but God has not. Nor has the foundation of our liberty.

On September 25, 1789, Congress passed the proposed Bill of Rights, including the First Amendment to the U.S. Constitution that enshrined religious liberty as our nation's first freedom. On that same day, Congress proposed and ultimately passed (three days later) a Joint Resolution of the following:

> *That a joint committee of both Houses be directed to wait upon the President of the United States, to request that he would recommend to the people of the United States a day of public thanksgiving and prayer to be observed by acknowledging, with grateful hearts, the many signal favors of Almighty God, especially by affording them an opportunity peaceably to establish a Constitution of government for their safety and happiness.*

As a response to that resolution, President Washington established our nation's first official Thanksgiving. His proclamation contained the following:

> *It is the duty of all Nations to acknowledge the providence of Almighty God, to obey his will, to be grateful for his benefits, and humbly to implore his protection and favor – and whereas both Houses of Congress have by their joint Committee requested me to recommend to the People of the United States a day of public thanksgiving and prayer to be observed by acknowledging with grateful hearts the many signal favors of Almighty God especially by affording them an opportunity peaceably to establish a form of government for their safety and happiness.*

The juxtaposition of these two events on the same day is stunning. Our Founders whole-heartedly supported the religious liberty guaranteed by the First Amendment while passionately supporting a public day that gratefully acknowledged our trust in Almighty God. It was no violation of foundational principles – in fact, just the opposite. As Washington stated: "It is the duty of all Nations to acknowledge the providence of Almighty God." It is our duty to do so today as well, while embracing the liberty provided by our first freedom!

THROUGHLY FURNISHED

The Founding Fathers saw the Lord's hand at work in building the structure of their government through the U.S. Constitution. As they stepped away from the Constitutional Convention, they sensed that the Lord had guided them throughout those sweltering four months in Philadelphia.

James Madison: "It is impossible to consider the degree of concord which ultimately prevailed as less than a miracle."

George Washington: The Constitution "will demonstrate as visibly the finger of Providence as any possible event in the course of human affairs."

Alexander Hamilton "For my own part, I sincerely esteem it a system which, without the finger of God, never could have been suggested and agreed upon by such a diversity of interests."

Others later reiterated this important truth.

Dr. Alice Baldwin wrote the following in her assessment of early U.S. history in 1928: "The constitutional convention and the written constitution were the children of the pulpit." It was Biblical literacy and sensitivity, and a firm trust in God, that had formed and shaped our nation's founding documents and foundational culture.

Furthermore, at a prayer breakfast recorded in *Time Magazine*, Supreme Court Chief Justice Earl Warren said the following in 1954:

> *I believe no one can read the history of our country*
> *without realizing that the Good Book and the spirit of*
> *the Saviour have from the beginning been our guiding*

> *geniuses ... Whether we look to the first Charter of Virginia ... or to the Charter of New England ... or to the Charter of Massachusetts Bay ... or to the Fundamental Orders of Connecticut ... the same objective is present: a Christian land governed by Christian principles.*

Warren was anything but a strong conservative. Nominated by President Dwight D. Eisenhower, Warren may be best known for being far more liberal of a justice than anyone expected. Yet, he recognized one important fact – our nation's foundation was undeniably built upon Christ.

Foundations are important, and Chief Justice Warren had no qualms about expounding upon what the American population already knew to be true – we were a land governed by Christian principles. That was the objective of our Founders, and they succeeded in building upon a foundation that standeth sure. It wasn't a nation built upon human geniuses, but by a Guiding Genius.

Chief Justice Warren went on to proclaim the following:

> *I believe the entire Bill of Rights came into being because of the knowledge our forefathers had of the Bible and their belief in it: freedom of belief, of expression, of assembly, of petition, the dignity of the individual, the sanctity of the home, equal justice under law, and the reservation of powers to the people ... I like to believe we are living today in the spirit of the Christian religion. I like also to believe that as long as we do so, no great harm can come to our country.*

A scriptural foundation gave our nation a strength and stability that was unmatched. "All scripture is given by inspiration of God, and is profitable for doctrine, for reproof, for correction, for instruction in righteousness: That the man of God may be perfect, throughly furnished unto all good works" (II Timothy 3:16-17).

We began, as a nation, throughly furnished. We existed through the decades, as a nation, because we were throughly furnished. We endured the difficulties, as a nation, because we were throughly furnished. We thrived, as a nation, because we were throughly furnished.

President Teddy Roosevelt wisely stated the following: "The teachings of the Bible are so interwoven and entwined with our whole civic and social life that it would be literally – I do not mean figuratively, I mean literally – impossible for us to figure to ourselves what that life would be if these teachings were removed."

We were designed as a nation that rested on a firm foundation and a trustworthy truth.

AVOIDING THE MAXIMS OF THIS WORLD

Noah Webster is known as the "Father of American Scholarship and Education." He was an author, an abolitionist, and an outspoken supporter of the Constitution. Later in his life, this Founding Father wrote two must-read books for children and adults alike:

- *The Value of the Bible and Excellence of the Christian Religion: For the Use of Families and Schools* (1834)

- *History of the United States* (1833)

Webster wrote the following:

> *The great difference between the maxims of the world and the doctrines of the gospel, is, that human opinions spring from pride, and tend to foster it; whereas the doctrines of the gospel teach humility, and self-abasement. The maxims of the world serve to encourage self-dependence in men, inducing them to rely on their own strength and resources for success, in business or policy, without seeking aid from the Almighty source of power. The gospel inculcates the opposite doctrine; it teaches that "God resisteth the proud, but giveth grace to the humble." It serves to make men humble, and to rely wholly on God for success, not only in spiritual concerns, but in the ordinary occupations of this*

world. In the pagan world, bravery and human efforts are everything; and God is nothing. In the Christian system, human strength is nothing, and God is every thing. In a Christian community then, all government should be founded on Christian principles or should be directed to support them; and to such a system God will give success. All governments of a different kind will produce, as they have ever produced, innumerable evils while they last, and will ultimately sink into corruption and be ruined. All history is a tissue of facts confirming these observations.

This Founding Father recognized the need to embrace humility and to shun pride. He recognized that this applies at the personal level and to the governmental level. He recognized that the former would bring grace and the latter would bring resistance. He also recognized that civil liberty flowed from the applied truths of Christianity:

Almost all the civil liberty now enjoyed in the world owes its origin to the principles of the Christian religion ... the religion which has introduced civil liberty, is the religion of Christ and his apostles, which enjoins humility, piety, and benevolence; which acknowledges in every person a brother, or a sister, and a citizen with equal rights. This is genuine Christianity, and to this we owe our free constitutions of government.

This nation was special because it didn't spring from the maxims of this world, but instead from the principles of heaven. The Founders recognized that human strength is nothing and that God is everything. The Constitution was derived from this key truth – it was the work of a Divine Providence and was crafted by those who trusted in Him!

CHAPTER 8

A SACRED CAUSE AND A SACRED FIRE

BY JOHN TEICHERT

Throughout the American Revolutionary War, General George Washington proclaimed that their struggles for liberty were a "sacred cause." By the time he took his inaugural oath on April 30, 1789, President Washington charged his fellow citizens to preserve the "sacred fire of liberty."

The Founders who assembled in Manhattan for the first inaugural address had succeeded in achieving the sacred cause of liberty and igniting the burning flame of the sacred fire of liberty. Each generation was responsible to fan those flames by following the "eternal rules of order and right, which Heaven itself has ordained."

Our nation's first inauguration under the Constitution provided a wonderful punctuation for this sacred cause while ensuring that the sacred fire of our Founders had its flames fanned as the nation launched into an uncertain future.

AN IMPORTANT TRAIN OF CONSEQUENCES

On April 16, 1789, George Washington left the comforts of Mount Vernon to make the trek to our new nation's capital in New York City. Two weeks later, he was to take the oath of office as our nation's first president. In his journal on that day, he wrote:

> *About 10 o'clock I bade adieu to Mount Vernon, to private life, and to domestic felicity, and with a mind oppressed with more anxious and painful sensations than I have words to express, set out for New York in company with Mr. Thompson, and Colonel Humphries, with the best dispositions to render service to my country in obedience to its call, but with less hope of answering its expectations.*

He was mindful of his limitations and appreciated the burdens of such a responsibility.

In the first line of his inauguration speech on April 30, President Washington stated the following as he trembled in the Senate Chambers of Federal Hall: "Among the vicissitudes incident to life, no event could have filled me with greater anxieties than that of which the notification was transmitted by your order, and received on the fourteenth day of the present month." He went on to admit that he was "peculiarly conscious of his own deficiencies."

These words and others demonstrate a man filled with humility as he accepted the mantle of responsibility that came with his new office. This battle-hardened veteran realized that leadership was a weighty burden that no single person could shoulder alone. He entered this leadership position with the spirit of a humble servant.

Humility prompts leaders to question their assumptions. It urges leaders to seek outside opinions and lean on wise counsel. It causes leaders to look outward and upward instead of inward. It fosters a reliance on others instead of oneself. It nudges a leader to prioritize relationships. It inspires the elevation of an organization's needs over personal needs. It motivates leaders with the thought that a single leadership shortcoming can cause an organization to stumble.

Humility prevents complacency. It stirs up passions that abhor stagnation. It suppresses self-satisfaction and self-sufficiency. It halts power-hungry careerism and cronyism. It clips the tendency to strive for personal gain.

In the end, humility carefully guides a leader and an organization towards an excellence that elevates everyone. It was such excellence that weighed heavily on the mind of our first president.

On April 23, 1789, George Washington arrived in New York City in preparation for his inauguration a week later. On that same day, the *New York Daily Advertiser* announced the following:

> *On the morning of the day on which our illustrious President will be invested with his office, the bells will ring at nine o'clock, when the people may go up to the house of God and in a solemn manner commit the new government, with its important train of consequences, to the holy protection and blessing of the Most high.*

In 1789, America stood on the brink of history. As the constitutionally based government was forming, the world was watching. After a long-fought battle against the world's superpower, and a stumbling of government under the Articles of Confederation, could this new experiment work? Much was riding on the outcome, and the subsequent train of consequences demanded an inauguration day that was bathed in prayer. The people recognized the need to commit their new government and fledgling nation to the holy protection and blessings of the Most High.

The humble spirit of America's first president, and the prayers of the people of the newly formed government, set the stage for a stunning three-part inauguration ceremony that overflowed with reliance on the Lord their God.

SO HELP ME GOD!

At our nation's first Presidential Inauguration, Robert Livingston, the Chancellor of New York, administered that oath to our nation's first president on the balcony of Federal Hall. Importantly, though, President Washington added a key phrase to the end of his oath – "So help me God!" This short phrase has since become the standard for all forms of public office. On that day, Washington recognized that he could only faithfully execute his office, and only preserve, protect, and defend the Constitution if he relied upon the Lord.

As Washington went inside to deliver his inauguration speech, the theme of trusting in God was interwoven into his profound remarks to the new government.

A SPEECH OF FERVENT AND HUMBLE SUPPLICATION

President Washington's first inaugural speech was as much of a sermon as it was a political address. Our first president acknowledged God, trusted God, and implored God. To Washington, omitting any of these would be peculiarly improper. During his speech, Washington stated the following:

> *Such being the impressions under which I have, in obedience to the public summons, repaired to the present station; it would be peculiarly improper to omit in this first official Act, my fervent supplications to that Almighty Being who rules over the Universe, who presides in the Councils of Nations, and whose providential aids can supply every human defect, that his benediction may consecrate to the liberties and happiness of the People of the United States, a Government instituted by themselves for these essential purposes: and may enable every instrument employed in its administration to execute with success, the functions allotted to his charge.*

President Washington found it proper to turn to God at the outset of his presidency, and to do so publicly. After all, his faith was fundamental to his character. Additionally, Washington knew that the new government urgently needed God.

There were plenty of concerns about the future of this new nation. Yet, Washington didn't want those assembled to linger on their human defects. Instead, he wanted them to turn to the trustworthy source of endless supply.

President Washington continued in his inauguration speech with the following:

> *In tendering this homage to the Great Author of every public and private good I assure myself that it expresses your sentiments not less than my own; nor those of my fellow-citizens at large, less than either. No People can be bound to acknowledge and adore the invisible hand, which conducts the Affairs of men more than the People of the United States. Every step, by which they have advanced to the character of an independent nation, seems to have been distinguished by some token of providential agency. And in the important revolution just accomplished in the system of their United Government, the tranquil deliberations and voluntary consent of so many distinct communities, from which the event has resulted, cannot be compared with the means by which most Governments have been established, without some return of pious gratitude along with an humble anticipation of the future blessings which the past seem to presage. These reflections, arising out of the present crisis, have forced themselves too strongly on my mind to be suppressed. You will join with me I trust in thinking, that there are none under the influence of which, the proceedings of a new and free Government can more auspiciously commence.*

Washington saw the uniqueness of the new nation. He couldn't suppress the overwhelming thought that it was formed by the blessings of God.

He saw the Lord's hand in every step that advanced towards colonial independence, revolutionary victory, and united government. To Washington, no people should have been more humbly appreciative or eagerly anticipative than the citizens of the newly formed United States.

Washington saw the past blessings as an undeniable sign of future blessings. The past victory presaged future success. The new president wanted citizens to live in humble anticipation by looking back at what God had done, and to build upon His foundation with His help. Washington yearned for the past to motivate and encourage them into the future.

In this stunning inaugural address, President Washington went on with the following words of wisdom:

> *I dwell on this prospect with every satisfaction which an ardent love for my Country can inspire: since there is no truth more thoroughly established, than that there exists in the economy and course of nature, an indissoluble union between virtue and happiness, between duty and advantage, between the genuine maxims of an honest and magnanimous policy, and the solid rewards of public prosperity and felicity: Since we ought to be no less persuaded that the propitious smiles of Heaven, can never be expected on a nation that disregards the eternal rules of order and right, which Heaven itself has ordained: And since the preservation of the sacred fire of liberty, and the destiny of the Republican model of Government, are justly considered as deeply, perhaps as finally staked, on the experiment entrusted to the hands of the American people.*

Our first president, battle-hardened and politically tested, understood the inseverable link between faithfulness and felicity. He recognized the tie between order and well-being. He clung to the connection between righteousness and welfare.

Washington rightly surmised that neither a person nor a nation could expect God's blessings if they disregarded their responsibilities towards Him.

President Washington closed his first inaugural address with the following:

> *Having thus imported to you my sentiments, as they have been awakened by the occasion which brings us together, I shall take my present leave; but not without resorting once more to the benign parent of the human race, in humble supplication that since he has been pleased to favour the American people, with opportunities for deliberating in perfect tranquility, and dispositions for deciding with unparalleled unanimity on a form of Government, for the security of their Union, and the advancement of their happiness; so his divine blessing may be equally conspicuous in the enlarged views, the temperate consultations, and the wise measures on which the success of this Government must depend.*

Washington's final remarks in the nation's first presidential inauguration were of humble supplication. He expressed appreciation to God for past blessings. He indicated dependence on God for future blessings. He accepted that their level of faithfulness would make the difference between future success and failure.

The rest of the government was sensitive to those same considerations.

RESOLVED

Prior to Washington's inauguration, Congress acted to ensure that the government would be founded on prayer, strengthened in prayer, and buoyed by prayer. On April 27, 1789, the Senate approved the following resolution: "Resolved, That, after the oath shall have been administered to the President, he, attended by the Vice President, and members of the Senate and House of Representatives, proceed to St. Paul's Chapel, to hear divine service, to be performed by the Chaplain of Congress."

Two days later, the House approved the same. In obedience to this Joint Resolution, Congressional records documented the following as the first act of the new government after Washington's inauguration speech of fervent and humble supplication: "The President, the Vice President, the Senate, and House of Representatives, then proceeded to St. Paul's chapel, where divine service was performed by the chaplain of Congress."

With a quorum of U.S. Constitution signatories present, the new government's first act, as required by Congressional resolution, was to attend a Christian church service that included prayers, scripture readings, and a message from the books of Psalms, I Kings, Acts, and III John. Recognizing that the success of such a new nation would rise or fall based on the Lord Himself, national leaders immediately embraced and demonstrated prayerful humility. They saw that their future hinged not upon themselves, but on the Lord. They wanted the world to know that their God was the Lord and they trusted in Him.

A GLORIOUS LIBERTY DOCUMENT

As the nation's founding period came to an end with the inauguration of President George Washington, it is important to look back on the source of our freedom and the core of our national strength. Eighty years ago, as world war ravaged the planet and as young Americans were deployed in heavy combat in every corner of the globe, Pastor Lynd Esch wrote these powerful thoughts about our Godly heritage while providing a stern warning if we were to ever wander from our firm foundation of trust.

> *One of the really great heritages of the American people is the heritage of noble ancestry. It is with a spirit of just pride that we point to their achievements in the growth and development of our democracy. They blazed a new trail in the wilderness; this was done, not only with their axes as they carved roadways across the continent from the eastern seaboard to the Pacific Ocean, but also with their freedom-loving minds. They blazed a new trail with mind and heart as they laid the firm foundation for our "land of the free and home of the brave."*

We must never lose sight of the fact that these men whom we honor were enabled to do great deeds because they had great faith. Their faith was in God. Belief in a God of justice and righteousness, a God of mercy and love, moved them to heroic deeds in the cause of freedom and liberty.

If we would preserve, extend, and perpetuate the ideals for which our fathers gave their all, then we too must be inspired by faith in their God. If the day should ever come when we should lose our fathers' God, if enough of the people of our land should definitely turn aside from His teaching, then we would we also lose our own and our children's freedom. May the God of our fathers inspire our lives to loyal service in protecting their ideals for those who shall come after us.

Some today, through a cancerous and twisted view of history, have a different view of our Founders. Thus, it is important to consider the provocative and powerful thoughts from Frederick Douglass, an amazing 19th century American orator, abolitionist, and women's suffragist. He was one of the greatest minds and speakers in American history. And as an escaped slave, he offers a unique view of the American experiment.

Douglass stated the following hard truth:

The American people, likewise, have made void their law by their traditions; they have trampled upon their own constitution, stepped beyond the limits set for themselves, and, in their ever-abounding iniquity, established a constitution of action outside of the fundamental law of the land. While the one is good, the other is evil; while the one is for liberty, the other is in favour of slavery; the practice of the American government is one thing, and the character of the constitution of the government is quite another and different thing.

There is an important nuance to be noted though. When it came to slavery and other shortcomings in our society, there was a major application problem with our founding principles and not an underlying systemic problem. In fact, Douglass said that "the Constitution is a GLORIOUS LIBERTY DOCUMENT" (emphasis provided by Douglass). He called our Founders "great men" and "brave men." He stated that "the fathers are entitled to the profound gratitude of mankind."

None of these thoughts overlook their sins, their tragic errors, or their serious shortcomings. Those are plain for all to see. But for Douglass and for us today, we must recognize the stunning brilliance of a government formed on an acknowledgement of the higher powers that are ordained of God. The Constitution and the Declaration of Independence can be considered GLORIOUS LIBERTY DOCUMENTS because they are formed on a Biblical bedrock – the ultimate GLORIOUS LIBERTY DOCUMENT.

The sacred cause of our 250-year-old experiment in liberty enjoys a transcendent power because of its firm foundation of trust and dependency.

SECTION 3

AN UNBROKEN SPIRIT OF ORGANIC UTTERANCES

The previous section intentionally expounds about the foundational years of the United States of America. It is deliberately thorough to demonstrate the consistency of the founding attitude throughout the period that led up to our nation's first inauguration. The overwhelming spirit of trust and dependency illustrates the basis for our society and emphasizes the relevancy of our national motto.

Yet, there is so much more to the active and persistent application of *In God We Trust* that played a pivotal role in the decades and centuries that followed our founding. The following stories provide a small body of additional evidence that points us back to our national and personal reliance upon Him. It is a small selection of historical, practical, and spiritual highlights that further demonstrate an important truth – our nation and her leaders have consistently made our national motto their personal declaration.

SPEAKING THE VOICE OF THE ENTIRE PEOPLE

BY JOHN TEICHERT

The case *Church of the Holy Trinity v. United States* was decided by the Supreme Court in 1892. This case centered around a law that prohibited foreigners from working in the United States due to a fear of foreign competition. As a byproduct of that law, foreign pastors were excluded from serving in the United States as well. Justice Brewer's unanimous majority opinion held that such a law did not apply to the ministry, in a large part because we were a Christian nation that would never prohibit foreign pastors from entering our land. Brewer wrote:

> But, beyond all these matters, no purpose of action against religion can be imputed to any legislation, state or national, because this is a religious people. This is historically true. From the discovery of this continent to the present hour, there is a single voice making this affirmation.

Justice Brewer went on to demonstrate this truth by the words and actions of our Founders and from the entirety of our society. Society had proved such a claim through its history and tradition.

In his written decision of the case, Justice Brewer laid out a lengthy body of historical evidence that demonstrated our national Christianity. He used charters, constitutions, oaths, and court records:

> *There is no dissonance in these declarations. There is a universal language pervading them all, having one meaning. They affirm and reaffirm that this is a religious nation. There are not individual sayings, declarations of private persons. They are organic utterances. They speak the voice of the entire people.*

Justice Brewer then outlined the Christianity displayed by our laws, our businesses, our customs, and our society. He drew evidence from the efforts of our charities and the works of our missionaries, finally coming to the following conclusion:

> *These, and many other matters which might be noticed, add a volume of unofficial declarations to the mass of organic utterances that this is a Christian nation. In the face of all these, shall it be believed that a Congress of the United States intended to make it a misdemeanor for a church of this country to contract for the services of a Christian minister residing in another nation?*

The organic utterances of this nation had spoken with the voice of the people. While this case has fallen out of favor in conservative judicial thought – seeing it as sociologically true, but legally false – it still provides a powerful marker of prevailing thought as the nineteenth century came to a close. The Court provided irrefutable social proof that we were predominantly Christian at our core and our trust rested firmly in our Lord and Saviour. Subsequent cases such as *Marsh v. Chambers* in 1983 point to similar elements of our nation's "unique history" and "two centuries of national practice" that punctuate this important social and historical truth.

CHAPTER 10

SHOWERS OF GRACE

BY JOHN TEICHERT

I n spite of these organic utterances, midway through the Nineteenth Century faithfulness in America was waning. It was said that "the whole country was on the very verge of volcanic eruptions of vice and political disaster." Like today, something needed to be done to spark a trusting return to God.

Jeremiah Lanphier was a Dutch businessman in New York City during this period of desperately needed revival. He had no theological or ministerial training but was well-regarded in his business and church communities during a time of change in the demographics of his lower Manhattan neighborhood. He felt led to serve Christ more fully with his life and answered the call to be a lay missionary for the North Dutch Church. On July 1, 1857, he shuttered his business and faithfully followed God's calling on his life.

A few months later he started a prayer meeting for businessmen, though his church board was initially dismissive and unenthusiastic about the idea. Lanphier advertised his gathering by putting the following placard outside a room in lower Manhattan on Wednesdays: "Prayer Meeting from 12 to 1 o'clock – Stop 5, 10, or 20 minutes, or the whole hour, as your time admits."

From a simple and inauspicious start, the Lord used this meeting in a mighty way. America at that time had gone through a recognizable cycle. It had seen great prosperity and had lost interest in God. Then their prosperity and stability started crumbling and they recognized their need to return to their first love. Lanphier's prayer meetings fostered and fulfilled this need.

Jeremiah Lanphier's fliers asked and answered:

> *HOW OFTEN SHALL I PRAY?*
>
> *As often as the language of prayer is in my heart; as often as I see my need of help; as often as I feel the power of temptation; as often as I am made sensible of any spiritual declension or feel the aggression of a worldly spirit.*
>
> *In prayer we leave the business of time for that of eternity, and intercourse with men for intercourse with God.*

The business of time needed to yield to more pressing matters. The prayer meetings offered the opportunity to focus on the business of eternity. Based on the results, such business was long overdue, greatly needed, and magnificently impactful.

God's presence is what gave this meeting, and others like it, their power. There was no centralized earthly authority. There was no earthly master plan. There was instead a single meeting, ordained by God, which prompted other meetings to spring up all around the country. God tugged on the hearts of others to replicate a focus on the business of eternity.

Lanphier's handbills also included a short poem entitled the "Benefits of Prayer." It included the following stanza highlighting a potent charge to return to a spirit of humility and dependency:

Depend on Him, thou canst not fail;
Make all thy wants and wishes known;
Fear not, His merits must prevail;
Ask but in faith – it shall be done.

But was the population ready to embrace a message of depending on Him?

Shortly after the beginning of the prayer meetings, the economy faced a sharp downturn known as The Panic of 1857, a financial crisis that began in New York City and quickly spread throughout the country. Banks and businesses closed, and people faced severe unemployment. While the conditions in those days seemed dire, these unique challenges created an urgent neediness for the truths of God, the prayers of the people, and the hope of the gospel. The economic downturn even gave people time to regularly attend the prayer meetings when a prosperous time would have otherwise deprived them of an opportunity to do so. God had orchestrated things perfectly for revival in their day, working all things together for good in accordance with His purposes.

Jeremiah Lanphier was joined by five others during his first lunchtime prayer meeting on September 23, 1857, as they trickled into the meeting during the allotted hour. The following week, there were a total of twenty prayer warriors and the week after that the number doubled to forty. As a result, Lanphier transitioned to daily meetings. The numbers kept growing and the spreading results were described in the following way:

> *Seeing the intense spiritual hunger and the need for more space, many pastors began opening their churches for morning and evening prayer and were astounded when their sanctuaries were filled with hungry seekers desiring to call on the name of the Lord.*
>
> *A spirit of prayer seemed to be unleashed from the Fulton Street meeting to the nation. Prayer meetings began springing up in Philadelphia, Boston, Washington D.C., Pittsburg, Cincinnati, Indianapolis, Chicago and in a multitude of smaller cities and rural areas.*

A small step of faith and a simple act of prayer ignited a huge movement of God that far exceeded the expectations of the participants while perfectly meeting the desperate needs of the day. God's power was not confined to a single weekly meeting in lower Manhattan. Unleashed by the spirit of prayer among His people that was prompted by an intense spiritual hunger, it spread throughout the land. The results were astonishing! God even used the U.S. Navy as a conduit for the spreading of His truth and an understanding of His trustworthiness.

A ship was docked in New York Harbor during this time as a conduit for recruitment of potential service members. As a result, sailors who would be sent throughout the U.S. Navy were influenced by the culture onboard a singular ship. And, in God's perfect way, this culture was impacted by Jeremiah Lanphier's prayer meetings.

In fact, sailors who had been influenced by the prayers on Fulton Street began a daily prayer meeting onboard the ship. As a result, the spreading impact of prayer in New York City had a direct impact in prompting prayer around the world. Specifically, prayers that began with Lanphier and a few other men had a direct link to the Ulster Revival of 1859 that gripped the entire British Empire. All of this transpired because Lanphier was faithful and God is sovereign! Lanphier's activities in his small corner of the world spread around the planet.

An individual from far away shared the following testimony that had spread far away from its origin:

> *I came from India, and I landed but yesterday. I have come all the way from that far distant land to see for myself what the Lord is doing in America. I am an Englishman by birth, but my home is in India. We have heard of the glorious outpouring of the Holy Spirit upon your Churches, and we have rejoiced at it with exceeding joy. We believe as you believe, that we stand in the first breaking light of a most eventful day – an era of greater displays of Divine grace in the salvation of sinners than the world has ever seen. We need faith that is equal to the times. We need confidence to ask great things of God, and we shall get great things. Ask little things, and we shall get little things. But ask mighty showers of grace, and they will be poured out like a flood upon us.*

This Christian came all the way from India to see the miracle of God for himself; a miracle that had been activated by dependent and humble prayer. He saw the desperate need for a miraculous moving of the Spirit of God that demanded faith that was equal to the times. He also provided a critical reminder to all of us on the importance of a confidence to ask great things of God and to avoid small faith that merely yields small results. He yearned for mighty showers of grace that would be poured out like a flood upon them.

CHAPTER 11

WITH THAT ASSISTANCE WE COULD NOT FAIL

BY JOHN TEICHERT

As President-elect Abraham Lincoln was on the verge of leaving his hometown of Springfield, Illinois, for Washington D.C. in 1861, the viability of the nation was in question. Lincoln, realizing the immense challenges he would face spoke the following words in what is now known as his Farewell Address:

> *My friends – No one, not in my situation, can appreciate my feeling of sadness at this parting. To this place, and the kindness of these people, I owe every thing. Here I have lived a quarter of a century, and have passed from a young to an old man. Here my children have been born, and one is buried. I now leave, not knowing when, or whether ever, I may return, with a task before me greater than that which rested upon Washington. Without the assistance of the Divine Being who ever attended him, I cannot succeed. With that assistance I cannot fail. Trusting in Him who can go with me, and remain with you and be every where for good, let us confidently hope that all will yet be well. To His care commending you, as I*

> *hope in your prayers you will commend me, I bid you an*
> *affectionate farewell.*

Lincoln's words from the Springfield Great Western Railroad Depot directly mirror John 15:5: "I am the vine, ye are the branches; He that abideth in me, and I in him, the same bringeth forth much fruit: for without me ye can do nothing."

He recognized that with the Lord he would not fail; with God he would bring forth much fruit. He also recognized that without the Lord he could not succeed; without God he could do nothing. It was a spirit of dependency that sustained him in the most-challenging years that he would face ahead.

Later, speaking against the sin of a self-sufficient spirit, President Lincoln stated the following:

> *Intoxicated with unbroken success, we have become*
> *too self-sufficient to feel the necessity of redeeming and*
> *preserving grace, too proud to pray to the God that made*
> *us.*

> *I have been driven many times to my knees by the*
> *overwhelming conviction that I had nowhere else to*
> *go. My own wisdom and that of all about me seemed*
> *insufficient for the day.*

Our sufficiency is of God and Lincoln knew it. He recognized the only place to go was to his knees to pray for God's blessings in a spirit of trusting dependency.

As a part of his 1863 proclamation for a Day of National Humiliation, Fasting, and Prayer, President Lincoln declared the following:

> *We have been the recipients of the choicest bounties of*
> *Heaven. We have been preserved, these many years, in*
> *peace and prosperity. We have grown in numbers, wealth*
> *and power, as no other nation has ever grown. But we*
> *have forgotten God. We have forgotten the gracious hand*

which preserved us in peace, and multiplied and enriched and strengthened us; and we have vainly imagined, in the deceitfulness of our hearts, that all these blessings were produced by some superior wisdom and virtue of our own. Intoxicated with unbroken success, we have become too self-sufficient to feel the necessity of redeeming and preserving grace, too proud to pray to the God that made us!

Lincoln rightfully recognized our national complacency. God had blessed our nation in amazing ways. He had brought us out of our Egypt. He had filled our wide-open mouths. Yet, we had not hearkened unto His voice. The only way to survive the Civil War was to get back to a trusting reliance on Him, and Lincoln was determined to lead the way.

CHAPTER 12

COMPLETING THE CIRCUIT

BY JOHN TEICHERT

orld War II created a strain on the entirety of American society. This two-front war tested the resolve of the American spirit and its reliance on a Holy God who would carry them through it. A few select examples illuminate the spirit of dependency that pervaded the uniquely American response to such a conflict.

Strength for Service to God and Country was written by pastors throughout the country during the war to distribute to American military members fighting for freedom around the world. Its introductory section shares the following about the purpose and content of this devotion:

> *This is your book. It is for you alone. Its purpose is to strengthen and sustain you in those troubled hours when you feel a Need that cannot be well put into words.*

> *All over this land you love – in the great cities, in smaller communities, in schools and colleges, and in houses of business – men have put aside the duties of the day to talk in type with you. They have done this gladly, eagerly – because they want to help – and because their hearts are filled with gratitude to America's soldiers, sailors, and marines.*

They are simple things, these messages. But then freedom, and righteousness, and love are simple terms, easy to grasp and comforting to cling to in troubled times. There is no need for fine writing, for big words and labored sentences when hearts talk with one another.

This devotional had particular power in its day because of the distributed nature of the message, for both the authors and the readers. Those words were given to military members who were deployed to face conflict in foreign lands that encircled the globe. Their dispersed readership provided an amplified message that spoke in personal and profound ways during times of great need. As a result, the network of authors and readers created a powerful bond of service that knitted the broader community together into one accord that supported, strengthened, and sustained while encouraging likeminded believers everywhere into a spirit of trust.

EVENTS IN THE HANDS OF GOD

Several years later, General Eisenhower made the decision to launch the aerial and amphibious invasion of mainland Europe on June 5, 1944 after carefully consulting with his advisors and subordinate commanders. The main invasion would start the following morning.

A year prior to that monumental decision, Eisenhower had led the successful invasion of Sicily. It was the first Allied foothold on the European continent that sparked their ability to claw back territory from the Axis powers in that theater.

In a spirit of trusting reliance and dependency that characterized the operation and its leader, General Eisenhower said the following: "There comes a time when you've used your brains, your training, your technical skill, and the die is cast and the events are in the hands of God, and there you have to leave them."

Throughout our nation's history, its well-being has been fostered by brains, training, and skill. Yet, in the end, the events have been in the hands of a trustworthy God, and there we must leave them.

ADVANCING FROM VICTORY TO VICTORY

Several months later, as Allied forces were driving east, General Patton displayed a similar spirit to Eisenhower's.

In December 1944, Allied success on the Western Front was far from assured. Though the Germans had been pushed back, they enjoyed a reduced front and shorter supply lines. Hitler saw an opportunity for a counterattack, though it necessitated bad weather to reduce the Allied airpower advantages.

As the Germans were planning this maneuver, General Patton's advance was hindered by bad weather. On December 8, 1944, Patton called Chaplain James O'Neill and tasked him with writing a prayer for improved conditions. General Patton approved the Chaplain's prayer and ordered 250,000 copies to be distributed to every man:

> *Almighty and most merciful Father, we humbly beseech Thee, of Thy great goodness, to restrain these immoderate rains with which we have had to contend. Grant us fair weather for Battle. Graciously hearken to us as soldiers who call upon Thee that, armed with Thy power, we may advance from victory to victory, and crush the oppression and wickedness of our enemies and establish Thy justice among men and nations.*

Following the drafting of a prayer card for fair weather, Chaplain O'Neill discussed the power of prayer with General Patton. Patton stated:

> *Chaplain, I am a strong believer in Prayer. There are three ways that men get what they want: by planning, by working, and by Praying. Any great military operation takes careful planning, or thinking. Then you must have well-trained troops to carry it out: that's working. But between the plan and the operation there is always an unknown. That unknown spells defeat or victory, success or failure. It is the reaction of the actors to the ordeal when it actually comes. Some people call that getting*

> *the breaks; I call it God. God has His part, or margin in everything. That's where prayer comes in. Up to now, in the Third Army, God has been very good to us. We have never retreated; we have suffered no defeats, no famine, no epidemics. This is because a lot of people back home are praying for us. We were lucky in Africa, in Sicily, and in Italy – simply because people prayed. But we have to pray for ourselves, too. A good soldier is not made merely by making him think and work. There is something in every soldier that goes deeper than thinking or working – it's his "guts." It is something that he has built in there: it is a world of truth and power that is higher than himself. Great living is not all output of thought and work. A man has to have intake as well. I don't know what you call it, but I call it Religion, Prayer, or God.*

Patton went on to say:

> *I wish you would put out a Training Letter on this subject of Prayer to all the chaplains; write about nothing else, just the importance of prayer. Let me see it before you send it. We've got to get not only the chaplains but every man in the Third Army to pray. We must ask God to stop these rains. These rains are that margin that hold defeat or victory. If we all pray, it will be like what Dr. Carrel said, it will be like plugging in on a current whose source is in Heaven. I believe that prayer completes that circuit. It is power.*

Patton knew that his army needed to complete the circuit. They needed God's power! There was only so much they could achieve by planning and working. The margin between defeat and victory was in God's hands.

Patton's Training Letter 5 was delivered to his force. It had "the approval, the encouragement, and the enthusiastic support" of Patton himself, providing a powerful focus "on the importance of prayer" to chaplains and commanders. The letter included the following:

Those who pray do more for the world than those who fight; and if the world goes from bad to worse, it is because there are more battles than prayers. "Hands lifted up," said Bosuet, "smash more battalions than hands that strike." Gideon of Bible fame was least in his father's house. He came from Israel's smallest tribe. But he was a mighty man of valor. His strength lay not in his military might, but in his recognition of God's proper claims upon his life. He reduced his Army from thirty-two thousand to three hundred men lest the people of Israel would think that their valor had saved them. We have no intention to reduce our vast striking force. But we must urge, instruct, and indoctrinate every fighting man to pray as well as fight. In Gideon's day, and in our own, spiritually alert minorities carry the burdens and bring the victories.

Patton's Training Letter 5 went on to state:

Urge all of your men to pray, not alone in church, but everywhere. Pray when driving. Pray when fighting. Pray alone. Pray with others. Pray by night and pray by day. Pray for the cessation of immoderate rains, for good weather for Battle. Pray for the defeat of our wicked enemy whose banner is injustice and whose good is oppression. Pray for victory. Pray for our Army, and Pray for Peace.

We must march together, all out for God. The soldier who "cracks up" does not need sympathy or comfort as much as he needs strength. We are not trying to make the best of these days. It is our job to make the most of them. Now is not the time to follow God from "afar off." This Army needs the assurance and the faith that God is with us. With prayer, we cannot fail.

Sure enough, under the cover of bad weather, a surprise and powerful German counterattack came on December 16, 1944 against a disadvantaged Allied force. Four days later, as the Allies were reaching the breaking point, the skies unexpectedly and uncharacteristically cleared.

For the next week, Allied airpower dominated the skies, resupplied the troops, and decimated the German forces. Cleared weather allowed brave Allied ground forces to turn the tide on the Germans.

At Patton's next encounter with Chaplain O'Neill, he said, "Well, Padre, our prayers worked. I knew they would." Chaplain O'Neill earned a Bronze Star medal for his prayer support as the Allied cause moved on from victory to victory.

DOSS PRAYED

A half a world away, combat medic Desmond Doss served as a member of the 307th Infantry Regiment as it fought for control of Okinawa. Doss' stellar service saw him become the first conscientious objector to receive the Congressional Medal of Honor.

As a combat medic, Doss served bravely and brilliantly. During a particularly intense battle, he tirelessly crisscrossed the bullet-laden battlefield for five straight hours to tend to fellow injured soldiers. He is credited with saving the lives of 75 men in the face of extreme risk.

Days before in a different engagement, Doss insisted that his company pray before the fighting began. Indeed, they did! During the fighting that ensued, Doss' company escaped with no casualties. When his company commander was asked for a written report that explained their success, he could provide no earthly explanation. Instead, he offered the simple two-word rationale – "Doss prayed!" Nothing else made sense or could explain the outcome. Like Eisenhower and Patton, Desmond Doss wisely understood the need for a trusting dependency on God.

CHAPTER 13

A MESSAGE WORTH SENDING

BY JOHN TEICHERT

As humankind watched the liftoff of Apollo 11 on July 16, 1969, they were mindful of the previous Apollo missions that had paved the way for this event through their own amazing accomplishments. Apollo 8, the mission that closed out 1968, provided its own noteworthy firsts. On that mission, astronauts Frank Borman, James Lovell, and William Anders became the first humans to travel beyond low earth orbit and the first to orbit the moon. They were humbled to be the first members of mankind to see the earth in its entirety.

As they orbited the moon on Christmas Eve 1968, they participated in the most watched television broadcast at that point in history. During that transmission they said the following: "We are now approaching lunar sunrise, and for all the people back on Earth, the crew of Apollo 8 has a message we would like to send to you." They then went on to read Genesis 1:1-10 out of the King James Bible.

Those three astronauts, with a vantage point unmatched at that point in human history, turned to the One whose vantage point is truly unmatched. From a perspective unrivaled by previous humankind, they turned to the One whose perspective is ultimately unrivaled. From a viewpoint that was breathtaking, they turned to the One who gave us breath. From a point of view that marveled at the entirety of earthly creation, they turned to the Creator of the heaven and the earth. They knew something that Americans have known since our founding, that the magnificence of God transcends everything else.

CHAPTER 14

THE ROCK ON WHICH OUR REPUBLIC RESTS

BY JOHN TEICHERT

On October 4, 1982, the following Joint Resolution (Public Law 97-280 and Senate Joint Resolution 165) was approved by the 97th Congress:

> *Whereas the Bible, the Word of God, has made a unique contribution in shaping the United States as a distinctive and blessed nation and people;*
>
> *Whereas deeply held religious convictions springing from the Holy Scriptures led to the early settlement of our Nation;*
>
> *Whereas Biblical teachings inspired concepts of civil government that are contained in our Declaration of Independence and the Constitution of the United States;*
>
> *Whereas many of our great national leaders—among them Presidents Washington, Jackson, Lincoln, and Wilson—paid tribute to the surpassing influence of the Bible in our country's development, as in the words of*

> *President Jackson that the Bible is "the rock on which our Republic rests";*
>
> *Whereas the history of our Nation clearly illustrates the value of voluntarily applying the teachings of the Scriptures in the lives of individuals, families, and societies;*
>
> *Whereas this Nation now faces great challenges that will test this Nation as it has never been tested before; and*
>
> *Whereas that renewing our knowledge of and faith in God through Holy Scripture can strengthen us as a nation and a people: Now, therefore, be it*
>
> *Resolved by the Senate and House of Representatives of the United States of America in Congress assembled, That the President is authorized and requested to designate 1983 as a national "Year of the Bible" in recognition of both the formative influence the Bible has been for our Nation, and our national need to study and apply the teachings of the Holy Scriptures.*

Interestingly, the Senate was controlled by the Republican Party during the 97th Congress and the House of Representatives was solidly controlled by the Democratic Party. Yet, despite a divided Congress, Public Law 97-280 sailed through both chambers with little to no resistance.

In this public law, Congress recognized "our national need to study and apply the teachings of the Holy Scriptures." Imagine that! They didn't stop by calling the Bible interesting literature. They didn't hold short by declaring the Bible intriguing philosophy. They didn't limit their proclamation by lumping the Bible into a grouping of other religious texts. They didn't just call for a casual reading of the Bible.

Instead, they proclaimed the national need to STUDY the Bible and APPLY it, renewing our knowledge of and faith in God in the process. Through such proclamation, the 97th Congress explicitly recognized that the Bible was not a book written by man, but by God. They recognized that its study was altogether profitable. They recognized that it would furnish us unto all good works, strengthening us as a nation and a people. And it was to be known as the rock upon which the Republic rests.

President Ronald Reagan provided the following proclamation to further emphasize these powerful truths:

> *Of the many influences that have shaped the United States of America into a distinctive Nation and people, none may be said to be more fundamental and enduring than the Bible.*

> *Deep religious beliefs stemming from the Old and New Testaments of the Bible inspired many of the early settlers of our country, providing them with the strength, character, convictions, and faith necessary to withstand great hardship and danger in this new and rugged land. These shared beliefs helped forge a sense of common purpose among the widely dispersed colonies – a sense of community which laid the foundation for the spirit of nationhood that was to develop in later decades.*

> *The Bible and its teachings helped form the basis for the Founding Fathers' abiding belief in the inalienable rights of the individual, rights which they found implicit in the Bible's teachings of the inherent worth and dignity of each individual. This same sense of man patterned the convictions of those who framed the English system of law inherited by our own Nation, as well as the ideals set forth in the Declaration of Independence and the Constitution.*

> *For centuries the Bible's emphasis on compassion and love for our neighbor has inspired institutional and governmental expressions of benevolent outreach such as private charity, the establishment of schools and hospitals, and the abolition of slavery.*

> *Many of our greatest national leaders – among them Presidents Washington, Jackson, Lincoln, and Wilson –*

have recognized the influence of the Bible on our country's development. The plainspoken Andrew Jackson referred to the Bible as no less than "the rock on which our Republic rests." Today our beloved America and, indeed, the world, is facing a decade of enormous challenge. As a people we may well be tested as we have seldom, if ever, been tested before. We will need resources of spirit even more than resources of technology, education, and armaments. There could be no more fitting moment than now to reflect with gratitude, humility, and urgency upon the wisdom revealed to us in the writing that Abraham Lincoln called "the best gift God has ever given to man ... But for it we could not know right from wrong."

Presidential Proclamation 5018 ended with the following:

The Congress of the United States, in recognition of the unique contribution of the Bible in shaping the history and character of this Nation, and so many of its citizens, has by Senate Joint Resolution 165 authorized and requested the President to designate the year 1983 as the "Year of the Bible."

Now, Therefore, I, Ronald Reagan, President of the United States of America, in recognition of the contributions and influence of the Bible on our Republic and our people, do hereby proclaim 1983 the Year of the Bible in the United States. I encourage all citizens, each in his or her own way, to reexamine and rediscover its priceless and timeless message.

In Witness Whereof, I have hereunto set my hand this third day of February, in the year of our Lord nineteen hundred and eighty-three, and of the Independence of the United States of America the two hundred and seventh.

Its priceless and timeless message, and the Savior whom it describes, is indeed the best gift God has ever given to man and the basis for an unbroken national spirit of trust. The organic utterances provide an unbroken lineage that continues today.

SECTION 4

A PERSONAL DECLARATION THAT PROLONGS

CHAPTER 15

REGARDLESS OF MERE MANPOWER

BY JOHN TEICHERT

"For the transgression of a land many are the princes
thereof: but by a man of understanding and knowledge
the state thereof shall be prolonged."
(Proverbs 28:2)

The historical evidence for a nation that has consistently trusted in God is weighty and compelling. Yet, as we consider our individual roles, it is easy to fall into the thought trap that a single person cannot make a difference. In a land of millions of people, what can one man or one woman do? How much will one vote count? How can one person sway the massive ship of state?

There are at least two things that we must remember when we start to slip into this line of thinking. First, we are to do our duty regardless of the outcome. Life is filled with situations where the results are left up to God. Our role is to be faithful, regardless of the situation, context, obstacles, or perceived benefits. Second, we never know when we are in a situation when one person does make a difference, when one man or one woman will have disproportionate results, when one vote tips the election, or when one person steers a new course. The potentiality of that situation in our next encounter demands that we act as if our faithfulness is the decisive factor. As John Quincy Adams famously said: "Duty is ours, results are God's."

The term *free rider* has important applications in economics and social science. It refers to someone who benefits from a resource without paying their fair share because others bear the burden. In many ways, American Christians have become free riders.

The Lord has blessed America throughout our history well more than we deserve. This disparity has become even more acute in recent days as the nation has invited cursings, not blessings, upon itself. The nation has been free-riding on God's grace, with a willful lack of appreciation for the Lord's unmerited favor. At the same time, those of us who have failed to regularly and fervently pray for our nation have been "free riding" on the faithfulness of those more dedicated to proper Christian citizenship.

The prayers of faithful citizens may have delayed the judgment of a longsuffering God on a nation that has invited His wrath. Their prayers may be all that separates America from a harsh and deserved fate. At the same time, their prayers may also be staving off an even more severe devolution of our society than that which currently brings sorrow to the faithful. Those who pray are paying the cost for the rest.

Free riders will always exist, but America Christians should not be numbered among them!

Yet, there is another reason we should remain faithful, even when we don't think we can make a difference – the power of the breakthrough. Nothing illustrates this point better than the story of Roger Bannister.

In the mid-1950s, the track and field world was awash with interest in breaking the four-minute-mile. It had never been done, and some were thinking that it was an impossible limit. World records had been within three seconds of the notable milestone since 1943 and kept creeping ever closer to the four-minute mark in the intervening decade. Yet, no one could break that magical barrier. Even though several men in 1953 and early 1954 were running within a few seconds of the mark, no one could surpass the challenge … until May 6, 1954.

On that day in Oxford, England, Roger Bannister ran a mile in just under four minutes. It could be done! Sure enough, 46 days later, Bannister's record was broken. By 1958, the record had decreased to below three minutes and fifty-five seconds. At that point, sub-four-minute miles had become the standard in the world of track and field.

Roger Bannister's breakthrough motivated others who were then aware that it was possible to do what was once thought impossible. David's breakthrough against Goliath did the same. Similarly, a single breakthrough by us can do the same in our land, but it takes our trusting faithfulness to trigger it.

Finally, there is a key element of our spiritual and practical context that must never be neglected. Pastor Richard Spann wrote the following to American soldiers in the midst of World War II:

> *One cannot measure manpower by counting troops or laborers in the factory, or the members on a church roll. Statistics can't record all of the resources. Scripture says that under certain conditions one shall "chase a thousand, and two put ten thousand to flight." It may not always be wise to insist on these proportions. But the principle is everlastingly valid. The physical strength of a man must always be added to the strength of his soul and his power for marshalling the resources of truth, righteousness, and love ... When armed with these, man finds himself working together with God and time, regardless of the mere manpower operating to the contrary.*

American Christians seem overmatched as we look at the secular forces aggressively aligned all around us. The other side is amply equipped with horses and chariots. They assertively advertise their might and power. They have erected sturdy walls and fortifications. They are numbered by the thousands and the ten thousands.

Relatively, our human resources are meek and meager!

Yet, we must not be deterred by a daunting tally of opposing manpower and a summation of statistics when we are characterized by a commitment to contend for truth, righteousness, and love. Most importantly, if we are aligned with the Lord then we can boldly face the battles that are raging in today's society.

The chapters that follow highlight essential elements of turning our national motto into our personal declaration that seizes upon the power of the breakthrough and avoids the fatal resignation that comes from being a free rider. God's plan is not dependent on mere manpower and is instead triggered by trusting faithfulness.

CHAPTER 16

WORDS OF FAITH THAT SAVE A NATION

BY BRAD WELLS

It is good to celebrate the faith spoken by the Forefathers of our nation, but if we expect to claim its power, we must own it ourselves. If we hope to save our nation, it is imperative that every American *personally declare* IN GOD *I* TRUST.

The fathers of our faith each had a personal encounter with God. Their failures and successes are preserved for us in order that we might learn from their mistakes and follow their examples.

Abraham, though imperfect in his trust in God, believed strongly enough to *command* his household to "keep the way of the LORD" (Genesis 18:19).

Isaac, seemingly less dynamic in personality and performance than his father, still blessed and *charged* Jacob about how to follow God and receive His covenant.

Jacob – yes, even conniving, deceiving Jacob – voraciously *clung* to the angel of the Lord to receive the blessing and declare it to the next generation.

"Give ear," Psalm 78 begins, "I will open my mouth ... I will utter dark sayings of old: which we have heard and known, and our fathers have told us. We will not hide them from their children, shewing to the generation to come the praises of the LORD, and His strength, and His wonderful works that He hath done ... That the generation to come might know them, even the children which should be born; who should arise and declare them to their children: that they might set their hope in God" (Psalm 78:1-7a).

Nationally, a silencing wave of cancel-culture may give us pause before we speak truth. Personally, a suffocating wave of failure-induced guilt may cause the words of faith to catch in our throats.

But, neither the cowardice of our fellow citizens nor the corruption of our finite character may be permitted to prevent us from rising *again* in the strength, grace, and forgiveness of our Great God!

You must confess your sin and be cleansed. The blood of Jesus cleanses us from all sin. It purges our conscience from dead works so that we might serve the living God. (Pray through 1 John 1:9 and Hebrews 9:11-14 right now.)

Words of faith that save a nation begin in our private prayer closet!

"Ye have not, because ye ask not" (James 4:2).

"Hitherto have ye asked nothing in my name: ask, and ye shall receive, that your joy may be full" (John 16:24).

What haven't we asked God for? What is He waiting for us to request so that He might spiritually bless and impact our homes and our nations?

A MIDNIGHT TRIP

It was midnight. My wife and I had just arrived in Washington, D.C. with our seven children the night before. We were there by a call of God, but we knew no one and had no place to live.

Not to worry, I had booked the Residence Inn in Carlyle on the Virginia side of the Potomac for two nights to get us started!

First things first: we attended a local church the morning and evening after we landed. Too cheap to pay for a rental car that held nine, we made two trips both morning and evening.

Now we sat wide-awake at midnight, our sleep clock defying the clock on the wall. Scrolling through Zillow, we noticed a house posted for rent for three to six months. "That's what we need!" Deborah exclaimed. "Something to just get us started."

Leaving our teenagers tucked safely in bed, we drove the few miles to the address. Unaware of how unusual the offer was and how odd we looked at nearly 1 a.m., we knelt in the driveway and asked God to give us this house as a starting place for our new venture.

With no rental history, no current driver's licenses, and no furniture, we moved into the beautiful little home on Apple Tree Drive that following Wednesday. It was on the windows of its sunroom that I wrote out with dry erase markers the plan to start – and even name – GraceWay Baptist Church of Capitol Hill.

You could say we did everything wrong in moving our family from the South Pacific to the epicenter of power for the entire world. But the accurate reality is we did everything we *could* and then *asked* the God of ALL power and supply to do what He could. And He did – exceeding abundantly above all we could ask or think!

We speak words of faith in our prayer closets, asking for cleansing for our failure and direction for our future.

However, if we hope to transform the culture around us and save our nation, we must also speak words of faith *to those we meet.*

The words of a song written by Kenneth Parker convict me every time I hear them:

I took Jesus as my Savior on a night not long ago,
And I found a perfect refuge where the stormy winds can't blow,

And now I want to tell the world lest one lost soul should die,
One I chance to meet, or even greet, Yet I let that chance go by.
Souls are dying, Souls we ought to win,
Souls who will reap in Hell the wages of their sin.
Oh, Christian, don't you care? Oh, can't you see them there?
Lose your wicked pride and pray and cry,
And never let a chance go by.

A young man stood lonely in a crowd. Having recently witnessed a horrific murder, he questioned all he had been taught about God and His goodness. "God, where are you in this terrible tragedy? How can I believe in You when you allow such evil in the world?"

"Excuse me, sir," a voice next to him said. "May I give you this?" He looked down to see a small paper with religious words written on it.

"Sure. Thank you," he replied, and the giver was swallowed up in the pressing throng.

Later that evening, as he shuttled to the metro station on a public bus, he struck up a conversation with the man sitting next to him. Sensing his confused state, the man began sharing Scripture with him. "Why does this man look familiar?" he questioned as the conversation grew deeper and more direct.

He pulled the paper out of his pocket with GraceWay Baptist Church on the cover and opened it again. "Is this you?" He asked the man, pointing at an exact replica printed on the inside.

"Yes," this surprised preacher said. "That is me in that picture. That paper is from my church. Where did you get it?"

"A man gave it to me earlier tonight," he replied, to the incredulity of them both.

An omniscient God had heard his prayer and led him to someone who could answer his questions from the Word of God. Not long after, he understood that the God who created the world also loved it enough to send His Son to die for every sin in it. He bowed his head and confessed

Jesus Christ as his Lord. In that simple act of faith, he believed and received the gift of eternal life.

If you are saved, you have been born again by "the word of God, which liveth and abideth for ever" (1 Peter 1:23).

We have God's promise in Romans 10:13, "Whosoever shall call upon the name of the Lord shall be saved." What a wonderful truth! All can be saved.

But, right after this inclusive statement, Apostle Paul gives a list of questions that convict us into decisive action and that dissolve all false notions that "being a good friend" and "accepting sinners as they are" are enough to lead them to repentance unto salvation.

"How then shall they call on Him in whom they have not believed? And how shall they believe in Him of whom they have not heard? And how shall they hear without a preacher?" (Romans 10:14-15)

In verse seventeen, Paul concludes his thought, "So then faith cometh by hearing, and hearing by the word of God."

Do we hope to affect our nation for good? Do we long to see teeming masses of new citizens embrace the faith of our Fathers? Do we weep for our children who are being enslaved to any number of vices?

The changing agent for our nation is the very "word of faith, which *we preach*" (Romans 10:8). Not just the word of faith which is in the Bible (though it is our source). Not only the word of faith which we think (though we should "think on these things"). But the word of faith which we preach!

To "preach" means to speak a truth with conviction. It means to speak a truth loud enough to be heard. It means to speak truth in a way that changes the way people think. It may be supplemented by various mediums such as the printed page or digital transmission, but truth's creative power is released through the vocal cords and diaphragm of one who has believed it enough to say it out loud!

Therefore, my brothers and sisters, let us come boldly before the throne of grace on behalf of our nation, confessing our sin, and asking for God to show His mighty hand to us and our children.

Then, let us to open our mouths boldly and "make known the mystery of the gospel" that we might save our nation before it is too late.

IN GOD I TRUST must be *personally spoken.*

CHAPTER 17

LIVING THE MOTTO

BY BRAD WELLS

It's easy to say something. It's quite another to *live* it. What does it mean to live out "In God I Trust"?

Let's review what trust means and expand our understanding of what trust is.

We trust what we *believe*. We believe what we *know*. We know what we *study*, *desire*, and *focus on*.

Trust sees and feels and leans upon something or someone proven to be reliable. This is why trust takes time to develop in a relationship.

Our relationship with our Creator is no different.

It wasn't always this way. At the beginning of creation, Adam and Eve walked with God unashamedly in the Garden of Eden. They enjoyed the sweet fellowship of unbroken trust every evening.

Then one day the enemy slithered into the garden of perfect joy and injected his poisonous lies into the open mind of the most vulnerable of the two. Instead of standing on the truth with trust, Eve leaned closer, sipped the seduction, and was deceived. Adam chose to support Eve in sin rather than rescue her with truth.

The first deception invited them to question what God had said. Perhaps God was not telling them everything they needed to know to be truly happy and fulfilled. If only they would eat the fruit, they could experience so much more! Like many people today, Adam and Eve believed *in* God, but they failed to *believe God*. This is a distinction that makes an eternal difference.

Secondly, who says the consequences of disobedience is death? And, what if it is? Perhaps death was not so bad after all.

Oh, but 6,000 years of corruption later, we know full well the effects of the serpent's damnable lies! Becoming as gods, knowing good and evil, did *not* make us happy. The very day they ate the forbidden fruit we all died to perfect, trusting communion with the Creator.

Eventually, Adam and Eve died physically as well. God had said, "In the day ye eat thereof ye shall surely die." Before the one-thousand-year "day of Adam" was over, Adam died at 930.

Everything God said was and *is* true. His word is trustworthy. Thanks be unto God, four thousand years later, God sent His unspeakable gift in the Person of His Son Jesus Christ. Through His perfect life He showed us how to live. Through His sacrificial death He took the payment for our sin upon Himself. Through His glorious resurrection He now has the power to reverse the penalty of sin for all humanity. We can be made one with God when we agree with His plan and confess Jesus as Lord to the glory of God the Father!

Yet even after we have been born again and our soul has been redeemed, we still have to drag around our old Adamic nature until our bodies are also redeemed. Sadly, and even unbelievably, the struggle with trusting our Creator continues even after salvation.

One moment we cry out in dedication, "Unto Thee, O LORD, do I lift up my soul. O my God, I trust in Thee!" (Psalm 25:1).

The next moment we find ourselves crying out in desperation, "Let me not be ashamed, let not mine enemies triumph over me! Yea, let none that wait on Thee be ashamed" (Psalm 25:2).

David was speaking of enemies that surrounded his kingdom. We, too, have real enemies that would try to defeat the kingdom of God within us. The society in which we live is no friend of God. The same slithering snake who tempted Eve, Satan, is now walking about as a roaring lion seeking whom he may devour.

However, the *closest* and most pervasive enemy of all is our old, unredeemed, anti-God, anti-truth nature! This is the part of Adam *in us* that is still lying to us about what God has said. It is the old pattern in our mind that will always lean away from His truth.

This is why we must *study*, *desire*, and *focus* on this mandate:

"Trust in the Lord with all thine heart; and *lean not* unto thine own understanding" (Proverbs 3:5).

What we *naturally* see, feel, and lean upon is what we can *actually* see, feel, and lean upon. It takes a *supernatural* transformation of our heart and mind to trust in the Lord.

It goes on to say in Proverbs 3:6, "In all thy ways acknowledge Him." The word "acknowledge" not only means "to know," but, even more than that, "to learn to know."

God wants you to be "filled with the knowledge of His will in all wisdom and spiritual understanding … being fruitful in every good work, and *increasing in the knowledge of God*" (Colossians 1:9-10).

That's a lot of words that basically says: GOD WANTS TO BE KNOWN! He desires to restore the intimate trust we once had with Him before sin duped us into walking away from Him.

Of utmost importance, you must repent of your sin and trust Jesus Christ as your only hope of salvation from sin and its penalties.

Once we are saved, however, there are three specific ways we can grow beyond "leaning on our own understanding" and begin "increasing in the knowledge of God."

KNOWING

The first way we grow is learning to KNOW GOD in His Word.

"Then said Jesus to those Jews which believed on Him, If ye *continue in my word,* then are ye my disciples indeed; And ye shall *know the truth* and the truth shall *make you free*" (John 8:31-32).

We can know some things about God through His creation. He is powerful. He is faithful. He is amazing!

But, if we want to be "filled with the *knowledge* of His *will,*" we must be filled with the *truth* of His *Word.* Simply put, read the Bible. Every. Day. When you falter and forget, get up and try again.

I'm not talking about listening to a podcast or reading a devotional. I am referring to opening the Word of God and reading its very words with your own eyes and brain. (White ink on black paper is the best method in my opinion. At the very least, it's the least distractive.)

My father-in-law, John Marshall, raised his ten children on daily Bible reading. It began when he and his wife, Leanore, noticed a change in the behavior of their eldest daughter, Julia, when she read a portion of the Bible in the morning. Instead of stubbornness, there was a pliable and gentle spirit. It eventually led to her understanding the Gospel and being born again.

John and Leanore decided to continue the experiment with every child who came along. The effect was the same. By the time my wife, their fourth child, was old enough to read, it had become the "law" of the land, or you could say, the "way" of the household. When the quiver of the family was finally full, each morning you could find twelve people with a Bible in their hand, "acknowledging Him" before they attempted any task for the day.

I, too, was given just such a discipline by my parents. The fruit of it is incalculable.

Let me hasten to say, it is *never* too late to begin the habit of reading God's Word daily. I had always thought, based on faulty research from the 1960s, that a habit is formed in 21 days. Well, maybe it can be formed in that timeframe, but we are now told it takes more like 60-254 days to solidify it. All the more reason to *start reading God's Word today*!

The point in daily Bible reading is to KNOW THE TRUTH. For it is through HIS knowledge that we are truly *made free* from the inside out.

BELIEVING

Secondly, if we hope to grow in trust, we must BELIEVE GOD IN PRAYER.

We are promised, "And all things whatsoever ye shall ask in prayer, believing, ye shall receive" (Matthew 21:22).

Do you see the qualifier? BELIEF. Again, we cannot believe something we do not know. This is why we begin by reading the Word.

Now, we must say it aloud to God. Pray it back to Him in the humility of total dependence upon His answer.

Have you ever felt like a caged bird, beaten back by some iron bars of unanswered prayer? There is a secret you must learn: *believe* when you pray, not with you *own* faith, but with the faith that is "not of yourselves: it is the gift of God" (Ephesians 2:8-9).

What has God told you in His Word? Pray with *that* knowledge. Believe it! There are souls, perhaps your own loved ones, who are outside of Christ, bound by the enemy, who will be set free when you *definitely* believe God! There are tasks just beyond your reach that, as you *doubtless* believe His promises, you will be empowered to achieve. There are wounds and addictions that, God will completely heal and overcome, as you *desperately* believe His power. *Pray*, my friend, *believing*!

GOING

Lastly, our trust in God will become strong as we GO IN POWER.

Do you want to see, feel, and lean upon One who has proven to be reliable for generations of faithful Christians? GO with the Gospel! I have been very intrigued with the wording of the Great Commission:

"Go ye therefore, and teach all nations, baptizing them in the name of the Father, and of the Son, and of the Holy Ghost: Teaching them to observe all things whatsoever I have commanded you: and, lo, *I am with you alway*, even unto the end of the world. Amen" (Matthew 28:19-20).

There is nothing—may I repeat, *nothing*—that exhilarates and fulfills your heart like giving the Gospel to another person.

I was on my knees in a small office directly across the street from the Supreme Court. "God, I am here. You called me and my family to come to this great city and 'cry against' its wickedness. I want to do that. Please show me how."

My phone rang. "Brad, would you like to go to the State of the Union Address tonight? I have an extra ticket," my friend Brian said.

"Would love to," I replied eagerly, "When and where should I meet you?"

"Well, I'm invited to the reception beforehand. It's mostly military, secretaries, and commanding officers and such. Would you want to join me there?"

I couldn't believe my ears! I had been working with the Marines at 8th and I just two blocks from the space our church rented for services. *During Bible study the night before, I told one of them that I wanted to meet the Commandant. "That's not possible, sir," our most faithful Marine, Nick Nosbisch, informed me. "Well, let's pray about it." And we had.*

"Uh, absolutely!" was my eager reply to Brian. I knew God had something special planned; I had just asked Him, and I had the distinct feeling He had heard.

I placed a business card, one with Scripture on it, in my pocket. (Being in D.C. for two years had taught me business cards were the handshake of Capitol Hill.) I had designed them to carry the Gospel as well.

Brian and I met up at the office of the Speaker of the House. The first person he introduced me to was the Commandant of the Marine Corps. I took a moment to brag on faithful PFC Nosbisch. Brian then introduced me to every head of every branch of our military. It was surreal, to say the least; and "exceeding abundantly above all" Nick and I had asked for!

After being guided through the proceedings of the evening, Brian said it was time to leave the balcony above the House Floor and head home. As we came down the stairs, the secret police said, "Sir, right this way," directing me towards the exit. "Stand right here, President Trump will be here momentarily."

I felt in my pocket. The Gospel business card was still there.

President Trump came through the doors and looked right at me. I stuck my hand out. He turned and shook the guy's hand next to me. My heart sank.

Then, the President of the United States turned back to me and stuck out his hand. I was ready. I said, "Sir, may I give this to you?" He took my card, looked at it, and said, "Thank you."

I watched him put it in his pocket and he was gone. Some years later I heard the verse on it quoted during a campaign speech. Who knows, perhaps he still has the card!

It was an honor to give the president a tract. But, my friend, it is an honor to give *anyone* a tract.

And if you're too afraid to give one to an actual person, start leaving them in prominent places: with your receipt at the restaurant, on the top of the gas pump, on a neighbor's front door …

In the privacy of your home, write out your testimony. Construct a few meaningful phrases, memorize them, and start practicing them when you're alone.

Ask God for strength to open your mouth in public. When He prompts you, *go*. Just say it!

The path to not only *saying* "In God I Trust," but truly *living* it is: 1) Knowing, 2) Believing, and 3) Going.

Read His Word. Pray. Speak out.

Every. Day.

CHAPTER 18

ENGRAVED

BY JOHN TEICHERT

Forty-two years after Lincoln signed into law the requirement that *In God We Trust* be engraved on all our coins, another debate erupted that had been spurred on by President Theodore Roosevelt. In 1907, Roosevelt established an executive order that stopped coins from containing this motto. His thought-provoking reasoning can inform our consideration of this motto today:

> *My own feeling in the matter is due to my very firm conviction that to put such a motto on coins, or to use it in any kindred manner, not only does no good, but does positive harm, and is in effect irreverence, which comes dangerously close to sacrilege. ... Any use which tends to cheapen it, and, above all, any use which tends to secure its being treated in a spirit of levity, is from every standpoint profoundly to be regretted. ... it seems to me eminently unwise to cheapen such a motto by use on coins ... In all my life I have never heard any human being speak reverently of this motto on the coins or show any signs of its having appealed to any high emotion in him, but I have literally, hundreds of times, heard it used as an occasion of and incitement to the sneering ridicule which*

it is, above all things, undesirable that so beautiful and exalted a phrase should excite.

The controversy didn't die down and Congress reinstated the motto. Yet, there is an important antidote to Roosevelt's concerns about cheapening our motto. We are to engrave it on our hearts, in our politics, and into our lives.

ON OUR HEARTS

The challenges we face today are no different than those experienced throughout human history. As God reminds us, "There is no new thing under the sun" (Ecclesiastes 1:9). As a result, our pitfalls follow a repeating pattern. The solution starts with an understanding that there is an enemy that is poised to pounce.

Our complacency and our fear, though, should prompt us to walk a narrow path of faithfulness between spiritual recklessness and paralysis. Meanwhile, our trusting vigilance provides an important steadying force: "Be sober, be vigilant; because your adversary the devil, as a roaring lion, walketh about, seeking whom he may devour" (I Peter 5:8). And as we trust in God, we arm ourselves to avoid defeat: "Unto thee, O LORD, do I lift up my soul. O my God, I trust in thee: let me not be ashamed, let not mine enemies triumph over me" (Psalm 25:1-2).

The Israelites provide a powerful reminder for us today. After escaping from Egypt, and seeing God part the Red Sea, they stood on the precipice of the Promised Land. God had already delivered them from the world's superpower. Before they crossed the threshold of success, they sent spies to scout out the situation. All came back acknowledging the grandeur of the land. Yet, ten of the twelve were transfixed by the challenges that awaited them. Instead of trust, they sowed seeds of doubt in their human ability to overcome the daunting task that awaited them.

Caleb and Joshua spoke up but were overwhelmed by the masses. In fact, the population's fear was so extreme that they conspired to murder God's trusting servants. Furthermore, the population started to create plans to return to Egypt and accept a future of renewed servitude. The results were thus recorded by Joshua:

"For the children of Israel walked forty years in the wilderness, till all the people that were men of war, which came out of Egypt, were consumed, because they obeyed not the voice of the LORD: unto whom the LORD sware that he would not shew them the land, which the LORD sware unto their fathers that he would give, a land that floweth with milk and honey" (Joshua 5:6).

The Israelites eventually made their way into the Promised Land. But instead of enjoying a direct trip from Egypt to a land that flowed with milk and honey, they wandered in the wilderness for four decades. When they did finally cross the River Jordan, they must have reflected on the fact that their lack of trust caused them to eventually get to where God intended for them to go, but with a long delay of hardship and heartache.

Our hearts are quick to trust in ourselves, but our actual self-sufficiency is not up to the task. God reminds us of the following: "Not that we are sufficient of ourselves to think any thing as of ourselves; but our sufficiency is of God" (II Corinthians 3:5). After all, our raw material comes from Him: "For who maketh thee to differ from another? and what hast thou that thou didst not receive? now if thou didst receive it, why dost thou glory, as if thou hadst not received it?" (I Corinthians 4:7) As a result, God plainly reminds us that our skills, our smarts, and our strengths are gifts from Him.

As a young Christian, I fully understood that God had given me the raw material of my life. After all, He had formed me from my mother's womb. Yet, I errantly retained a bit of credit for my situation in life. After all, while God had given me much, I had worked hard and wisely to develop it. As a result, God deserved some of the credit, but so did I. It was around that point in my spiritual journey that the Lord confronted me with the following from the Apostle Paul:

"For I am the least of the apostles, that am not meet to be called an apostle, because I persecuted the church of God. But by the grace of God I am what I am: and his grace which was bestowed upon me was not in vain; but I laboured more abundantly than they all: yet not I, but the grace of God which was in me" (I Corinthians 15:9-10).

Wow! Paul shares with us that his motivation to work hard was a God-given gift.

That means that while God deserves full credit for our raw material, He also deserves full credit for the ability to develop that raw material. Our relationships, our circumstances, our opportunities, and even our motivations are from Him. All our sufficiency is from Him and this truth of trusting in God must be engraved in our hearts.

IN OUR POLITICS

Speaking to President Lincoln about the Civil War, a Christian minister mentioned that he "hoped the Lord was on our side." Lincoln wisely responded: "I know that the Lord is always on the side of the right. But God is my witness that it is my constant anxiety and prayer, that both myself and this nation should be on the Lord's side."

This nation will not prevail over the challenges of the day because the Lord is on our side. Instead, we will only prevail if we are on His side. Christian Americans will not prevail over ungodly forces because the Lord is on our side. Instead, we will only prevail if we are on His side. Conservative Christians will not prevail against cultural progressives because the Lord is on our side. Instead, we will only prevail if we are on His side.

We must spend far less time assuming that God is on our side, and far more time ensuring that we are on His side. We must not presume that God will side with us and instead strive to perfectly side with Him. We must not assume His alignment but instead assure our alignment.

In our communal and collective endeavors – churches, neighborhoods, sports leagues, schools, workplaces, and governments – we are to engrave a trust in God into the fabric of our activities.

INTO OUR LIVES

The rubber meets the road when we make these concepts practical and tangible. The following eight items give traction to trust. Beware though, they buck the trends of societal norms and standard practices.

1) Trust in God even when it is against your flesh or the norms of the prevailing culture.

In August of 2018 I had just pinned a single star onto each of the shoulders of my uniform. I was now a brigadier general and had just started a new leadership job as the commander of Edwards Air Force Base – a place known as the Center of the Aerospace Testing Universe. During my first full week on the job, a very public attack questioned my character and threatened my future.

An organization that pounces on Christians in the military had their sights set on me. They must have been tracking me all along, and as soon as I became a more public target as a one-star general they launched their attack that included a 22-page letter to the Secretary of Defense suggesting that I should be fired and imprisoned. They pushed articles to the *Los Angeles Times* and *Newsweek* that further supported their claims. One of their slogans was: "General Teichert should be doing time behind prison bars, not commanding a Wing wearing a general's stars." I have to admit it's a bit catchy, but not exactly what I was hoping for during week one on the job.

What was my crime? It must have been something egregious for such an attack. In reality, it was rooted in a ministry I had launched five years prior that simply encouraged Christians to pray for our nation and our leaders at lunchtime (PLUS, or prayatlunch.us). How dare I do such a thing?!?!

As I was settling into my new position, it was a bit of shock and awe. After all, I was new in my job and trying to establish my credibility as a servant leader with a focus on our amazing team and our critical mission. That evening, I went home and we had a family conversation about this precarious situation. We prayed about it. And while my flesh wanted to lash out at my attacker, God brought a counter-cultural verse to my mind and my heart:

"But I say unto you, Love your enemies, bless them that curse you, and do good to them that hate you, and pray for them which despitefully use you and persecute you" (Matthew 5:44).

There may be nothing that runs more counter to the ways of the world than these words from our Saviour! I've done my best to put them into practice ever since then. In fact, I go out of my way to pray daily for the leader of the organization that attacked me. I did so earlier today before I typed this section.

How did it work out? First, God gave me a peace about the situation almost immediately. Second, God used the situation to bring national-level attention to my ministry in a way that only He could. That organization had meant it for evil, but God had meant it for good (Genesis 50:20), and the number of viewers to my website in one week eclipsed the previous five years combined. Third, I felt the prayerful love and encouragement of believers around the world who reached out in support. I even enjoyed the superb wingmanship of media personalities, like my friend Todd Starnes at Fox News, who quickly engaged on my behalf. Fourth, the Department of Defense quickly investigated me, determined that I had done nothing wrong, and told me that I could continue with my ministry. Praise God!

There is a bit more to the story. In early 2021, the presidential administration transitioned to one that was hostile to Christians and conservatives in the military. While my career was skyrocketing up to that point and while I had done nothing that had broken any rules, regulations, laws, or policies, the new administration was intent on weeding out faith-filled leaders like me. It was an ideological purge that didn't make the newspapers because big media was aligned with the administration. As a result, while serving in a position that was already designated for a 2-star general, instead of being promoted I was asked to retire.

It still stings a little bit, but I'm excited to see how God will continue to use that situation for His good. In the meanwhile, I will strive to trust in God even when it is against my flesh or the norms of our prevailing culture.

2) Trust in God even when it doesn't make any sense.

There is an important truth to consider whenever we are tempted to doubt God – who are we to believe that our perspective is sufficient to trump God's truths? After all, even the most globally capable among us only benefit from a myopic view of our circumstances. We are stunningly finite while God is supremely infinite. His omniscience, His omnipresence, and His omnipotence make our pride-filled cosmopolitan strivings simply sophomoric. Whenever you are tempted to trust yourself when circumstances seem to supersede your trust in God, fall back on the following:

"For my thoughts are not your thoughts, neither are your ways my ways, saith the LORD. For as the heavens are higher than the earth, so are my ways higher than your ways, and my thoughts than your thoughts" (Isaiah 55:8-9).

"Trust in the LORD with all thine heart; and lean not unto thine own understanding. In all thy ways acknowledge him, and he shall direct thy paths" (Proverbs 3:5-6).

His ways are always higher than our ways and we must never rest on our own understanding! As a result, we are to trust in Him even when it doesn't make any sense.

3) Trust in Him even when you think you have a reasonable work-around.

Abram and Sarai had been promised a child that would carry on an unmatched familial legacy. Yet as they aged, they were concerned that the odds of procreation were growing dim. Thus, they devised a trustless and faithless work-around:

"Now Sarai Abram's wife bare him no children: and she had an handmaid, an Egyptian, whose name was Hagar. And Sarai said unto Abram, Behold now, the LORD hath restrained me from bearing: I pray thee, go in unto my maid; it may be that I may obtain children by her. And Abram hearkened to the voice of Sarai" (Genesis 16:1-2).

How did it work out for them? They had a child, but it was not part of God's plan. And their "life hack" has severe ramifications for us today.

As a part of current portfolio, I speak frequently on national security and international affairs topics. I also am a regular commentator on NewsNation and Fox News. And if you looked at the hundreds of interviews I've done during the last few years, you would see a common trend – the majority of them are related to on-going chaos in the Middle East. Most of my media engagements center on nations like Iran and Israel, and groups like Hamas, Hezbollah and the Houthis. And the chaos has a singular root cause – Abram's and Sarai's decision to diverge from God's plan via their own seemingly brilliant work-around. It didn't work out well for them and it isn't working out well for us.

It is a great reminder that we are to trust in God even when we think we have a reasonable work-around.

4) Trust in Him even when it could be costly.

There is an interesting transition in Hebrews 11 – a chapter commonly known as the Hall of Fame of Faith. Throughout the chapter, God's people accomplish great things by faith. Abel, Enoch, Noah, Abraham, Isaac, Jacob, Sarah, Joseph, Moses and his parents, and Rahab all get specific mention for the magnificent and heroic things they were able to do by trusting in God. But it doesn't stop with them. Starting in verse 32, there are many more who follow in their path:

"And what shall I more say? for the time would fail me to tell of Gedeon, and of Barak, and of Samson, and of Jephthae; of David also, and Samuel, and of the prophets: Who through faith subdued kingdoms, wrought righteousness, obtained promises, stopped the mouths of lions. Quenched the violence of fire, escaped the edge of the sword, out of weakness were made strong, waxed valiant in fight, turned to flight the armies of the aliens. Women received their dead raised to life again …" (Hebrews 11:32-35a).

At this stage, I am convinced that I want to be a part of this legacy. Their exploits are incredible, and the outcomes are encouraging. Yet, in the middle of verse 35, it takes a turn:

"… and others were tortured, not accepting deliverance; that they might obtain a better resurrection: And others had trial of cruel mockings and scourgings, yea, moreover of bonds and imprisonment: They were stoned, they were sawn asunder, were tempted, were slain with the sword: they wandered about in sheepskins and goatskins; being destitute, afflicted, tormented; (Of whom the world was not worthy:) they wandered in deserts, and in mountains, and in dens and caves of the earth" (Hebrews 11:35b-38).

Yikes! Maybe such a legacy isn't for me.

This abrupt transition provides an important reminder for all of us – faithfully following God may not work out for us temporarily. Yet, pursuing God's path for us is always a part of His plan. It is a poignant reminder that we are to trust in God even when it could be costly.

5) Trust in God even when avoidance seems like an easy way to escape.

Many among us are procrastinators. As someone who loves to be ahead of the curve and ahead of schedule, I can't understand this particular temporal temptation. Yet, like all of us, sometimes I use strategic procrastination to put off the things that I know God wants me to do that seem challenging or onerous. These can be put off until tomorrow … and the next day … and the next day … and the next.

When I do so, it isn't a simple problem. It's something far worse than that: "Therefore to him that knoweth to do good, and doeth it not, to him it is sin" (James 4:17).

Spiritual procrastination is sin! Therefore, this verse must compel us to trust in God even when avoidance seems like an easy way to escape.

6) Trust in God even when you are fearful.

Fear on the verge of the Promised Land paralyzed the Israelites. Though it was universally known as a land that flowed with milk and honey, it also was populated by a formidable adversary. Their unwillingness to trust in God caused them to wonder in the wilderness for forty unnecessary, wasteful, challenging years. Eventually they got to where they belonged, but their fear caused them to be delayed for four long decades.

"Have not I commanded thee? Be strong and of a good courage; be not afraid, nether be thou dismayed: for the LORD thy God is with thee whithersoever thou goest" (Joshua 1:9). These were not hollow words from Moses's successor. They were a necessary charge to a people whose lack of trust had melted away their strength and courage. Similarly, they are a necessary charge to us today, and a major motivation to trust in God even when we are fearful.

7) Trust in God even when it takes overwhelming belief and prayer to believe.

In my life, I have been consistently warned against using circular logic. In writing or speaking, such a logical fallacy erodes credibility and destroys the foundation of a successful argument. Yet, the following story about our Saviour seems to rely on such a shortcoming:

"Jesus said unto him. If thou canst believe, all things are possible to him that believeth. And straightway the father of the child cried out, and said with tears, Lord, I believe; help thou mine unbelief" (Mark 9:23-24).

For all of us, we go through periods of waning belief, trust, and faith. When our well is running dry, Jesus reminds us that taking a determined step forward in faith can provide the antidote to a lack of trust and the tonic that can steel our belief.

Thus, it is not circular logic but a principle of faith that helps us maintain momentum even when we feel like stagnating in faithlessness. Deliberate belief yields derivative faith, and it is a key reason for us to trust in God even when it takes overwhelming belief and prayer to believe.

8) Trust in God even when it seems hopeless and helpless.

There was no greater time of despair for the human condition than during the crucifixion of Jesus. The future seemed bleak and hope had all but evaporated. The Saviour had been slain, and the King had been executed. The Bible records the following:

"Ye men of Israel, hear these words; Jesus of Nazareth, a man approved of God among you by miracles and wonders and signs, which God did by him in the midst of you, as ye yourselves also know: Him, being delivered by the determinate counsel and foreknowledge of God, ye have taken, and by wicked hands have crucified and slain" (Acts 2:22-23).

He was dead! Yet, the Bible goes on to provide a quick moment of miraculous recovery:

"Whom God hath raised up, having loosed the pains of death: because it was not possible that he should be holden of it" (Acts 2:24).

In a few short days and a few brief words, Christ went from dead to alive. He went from crucified to arisen. Christ loosed the pains of death in the biggest comeback in human history!

Every year, during the celebration of Christ's resurrection, I watch a video of one of my favorite songs from a couple of my favorite musicians – Daniel Hopkins and Freddy Kearney. I recommend you check it out.

My favorite set of lines are as follows:

His enemy, his ancient foe,
Content the dead was done.
Stood upon the battlefield,
convinced that he had won.
As Satan rose in triumph,

to put away his sword.
From somewhere in the darkness,
came the voice he'd heard before …
I WILL ARISE! I WILL ARISE!
Like the sun at dawn's first light,
I WILL ARISE!
You can bury me that day,
Seal the tomb and turn away,
But the Power of the grave will be denied.
I WILL ARISE!

Christ is a turn-around master. He is the comeback King! Not just on Calvary, but at every place, and every time, for all who believe. He turns despair into hope and helplessness into transformation. Our Saviour provides the most definitive reason why we must trust in God even when our situation seems hopeless and helpless! It provides the perfect punctuation to ensure that we engrave *In God We Trust* into our lives!

CHAPTER 19

IS GOD DEAD?

BY JOHN TEICHERT

"Then came the word of the Lord unto Jeremiah,
saying, Behold, I am the LORD, the God of all flesh: is
there any thing too hard for me?" (Jeremiah 32:26-27)

"And the LORD said unto Abraham, Wherefore
did Sarah laugh, saying, Shall I of a surety bear a
child, which am old? Is any thing too hard for the
LORD? At the time appointed I will return unto thee,
according to the time of life, and Sarah shall have a son"
(Genesis 18:13-14).

"I know that thou canst do every thing, and that no
thought can be withholden from thee" (Job 42:2).

Sojourner Truth was born a slave with the name Isabella Baumtree. She accepted Christ as her Saviour in her early 30s shortly after escaping from the inhumane bondage of slavery, and became an influential American abolitionist, women's rights activist, speaker, and author.

In 1847, Truth attended an event featuring the prominent speaker and abolitionist Frederick Douglass. That night, Douglass was uncharacteristically pessimistic about the prospects for the eradication of slavery in the United States, and Truth could not sit silently by and allow such a discouraging tone. In the midst of Douglass' speech, she stood to her feet and proclaimed three powerful words: "Is God dead?"

This rhetorical question with an obvious answer of NO quickly snapped Douglass from his pessimism and changed the tone of the entire meeting. It also became a rallying cry for the abolitionist movement in America and the cause of freedom for all people.

As we consider the challenging conditions of our day, we too might find ourselves slipping into an attitude of uncharacteristic pessimism about our future. When we do, we must stand to our feet and declare a similar sentiment to Truth's: "Is God dead?" As we remind ourselves of the obvious answer of NO, it should quickly snap us from our pessimism and change the tone of our entire environment. In fact, it should be a rallying cry for our Christian movement in America and the cause of freedom for all people as we put our trust into action in a society that desperately needs us to engage.

FOR SUCH A TIME

Esther had found favor with the king, her husband. As the decree went out to destroy the Jews, Mordecai called upon Esther to act for the betterment of her people. His challenge to Esther was simple – it is possible that the entire reason she had been placed in the palace at that time was to act with courage and creativity – "who knoweth whether thou are come to the kingdom for such a time as this?" (Esther 4:14b). If she did not, then she would miss God's purpose in her life and the blessings of God's plan would pass her by. Her inaction would be the worst course of action.

This challenge became an overwhelming burden to me and a call to action. It prompted me to launch the PLUS ministry (prayatlunch.us) in 2013.

It is possible that I had been placed in this position at this time to pray and encourage others to pray. The entirety of my background and experiences may have been preparation for this calling. If I failed to act, then I would risk missing God's purpose for my life and the blessings of God's plan would pass me by. My inaction would be the worst course of action.

Yet, this challenge goes far beyond the individual level, and it should be a broader call to action for all American Christians. It is possible that we have been placed in our positions in this nation to wrestle America back to godliness through our faithful prayers and trusting actions. If we fail to act, we may miss God's purpose for our lives and the blessings of God's plan may pass us by. Our inaction would be the worst course of action.

Upon God's second call to him, Jonah answered and complied (Jonah 3:1-3). The difference between the first and the second call was a little bit of time and a lot of turmoil … for Jonah himself. In the interval between God's first and second calls, Jonah experienced a tempestuous storm, he put those around him in peril, he lost a lottery, he faced condemnation from his shipmates, he was cast into the sea, he was swallowed by a great fish, and he was vomited onto dry ground. In the end, God's will was done despite Jonah's initial disobedience.

God doesn't need us to fulfill His will for our land. Yet like Jonah, if we refuse to answer God's call then we will be the ones who suffer the most. Indeed, our refusal to arise to God's call in our land could cause us personal turmoil. As Mordecai reminded Esther, without her "then shall there enlargement and deliverance arise to the Jews from another place; but thou and thy father's house shall be destroyed" (Esther 4:14).

With all the attention on Esther 4:14, we must not miss the power of verse 16. Convicted by Mordecai's words, Esther sets forth a plan to implement her unique role in her time and place. She is convinced that she is doing the right thing through her bold and faith-filled stand, but in verse 16 she acknowledges the risk and that the results are left up to God. Undeterred, she takes the large and trusting step of faith regardless of the potential consequences. Faithfully and not fatalistically, she walks into the unknown, boldly acknowledging: "and if I perish, I perish."

Shadrach, Meshach, and Abednego responded in a similar way, engaging in a unique role in their time and place. They were convinced that they were doing the right thing via their bold and faith-filled stand, but in Daniel 3:18 they acknowledge the risk and that the results are left up to God. Undeterred, they take a large step of faith regardless of the potential consequences. Faithfully and not fatalistically, they walk into the unknown, boldly acknowledging: "but if not … we will not serve thy gods."

We need American Christians to follow this path today – being believers who stand up and speak out. We have been placed here with unique roles in our time and our place. We must do the right thing via a bold and faith-filled stand in our situations while acknowledging the risk and that the results are left up to God. Undeterred, we must take large and trusting steps of faith regardless of the potential consequences. Faithfully and not fatalistically, we must walk into the unknown, boldly accepting the challenges through words of faith like Isaiah's: "Here am I, send me" (Isaiah 6:8).

We need more American Christians who will act like Isaiah. Before he even knew what the Lord wanted him to do, Isaiah was a volunteer. He didn't wait for others to take the lead; he took it himself.

It is simplistic to pinpoint widespread revival as the solution to our national problems. It is easy to passively expect others to correct our culture. It is a sterile platitude to demand a return to the values of our Forefathers. It is agnostically academic to sit ideally by and critique the failures of our population. It is ignorantly idealistic to expect change without individual effort.

It is naïve to presume change … apart from our involvement. Revival begins at the personal level. Change originates through individual initiative. Values shift when people consistently demonstrate them in their own lives.

Groups are comprised of individuals. *We* is made up of *me*; *us* is made up of *you*. If *I* don't get to work, then there is nothing *we* can do. If the Lord can't count on *you*, then He can't count on *us*. American Christians can only make a difference if we are composed of individuals who will say "Here am I; send me."

IF MY PEOPLE ...

"If my people, which are called by my name, shall humble themselves, and pray, and seek my face, and turn from their wicked ways; then will I hear from heaven, and will forgive their sin, and will heal their land" (II Chronicles 7:14).

We may be only one small word away from the Lord healing our land. The word IF is a simple conjunction that introduces a conditional clause. Though originally provided as a part of God's covenant with Israel, this verse introduces a contingent promise from the Lord that must inform us today. Based on the rules of logic and grammar, and its application to our situation today, the Lord WILL heal our land IF we meet the four conditions outlined in the first half of this verse. IF the conditions are met, then the outcome is certain. Yet, meeting the conditions is up to us.

So, what happens IF we fail to meet those conditions? This verse and the rules of logic and grammar do not prevent the Lord from fulfilling this promise without us. Yet, the use of the word IF carries with it a strong implication. In fact, *The Britannica Dictionary* includes the following definition of IF: it is "used to say that something MUST happen BEFORE another thing can happen. (emphasis added)" In other words, the conditions are necessary for the outcome to be met ... IF not, then not.

Christians are left with two choices: 1) meet the contingencies and be assured of the outcome, or 2) fail to meet the contingencies and risk an uncertain outcome at best or preclude a positive result at worst. It is far better to travel down the path of IF instead of risking a continuation of the status quo that is characterized by IF NOT.

Revival and healing will not come from government. Revival and healing will not come from entertainment. Revival and healing will not come from the courts. Revival and healing will not come from politics. Revival and healing will not come from the media. Revival and healing will not come from policies and programs.

Instead, revival and healing will only come from God as the result of the trusting obedience of His people. God is calling you; He is calling me. We are His people, and the responsibility for revival and healing is ours alone. IF revival and healing never come, it is not the fault of the world. It is our fault.

We must look no further than the mirror to determine the solution to our nation's problems!

RENDING OUR HEARTS

"Therefore also now, saith the LORD, turn ye even to me with all your heart, and with fasting, and with weeping, and with mourning: And rend your heart, and not your garments, and turn unto the LORD your God: for he is gracious and merciful, slow to anger, and of great kindness, and repenteth him of the evil" (Joel 2:12-13).

Are American Christians really concerned about the direction of our nation, or do we just enjoy complaining about our nation's drift from Christ within the safety of our social circles? The former would be accompanied by the rending of our hearts. The latter would be accompanied by a public pose akin to the rending of our garments. The former follows the Lord's commands. The latter reinforces our public piety. We can expect the former to foster conditions for revival, while the latter promotes conditions that will further our continued drift from Christ.

Our God wants us to invest ourselves in His work in our land. He wants our hearts to pay a modest down payment before He pays off the balance. He wants us to turn to Him with all our hearts, with fasting, weeping, and mourning. When we do so, then we create fertile conditions for Him to demonstrate His amazing grace, mercy, patience, and kindness that can change our direction. In a time like this, the mere rending of our garments will simply not do.

CHAPTER 20

SUPREME PRAYER

BY JOHN TEICHERT

"And I sought for a man among them, that should
make up the hedge, and stand in the gap before me for
the land, that I should not destroy it: but I found none.
Therefore have I poured out mine indignation upon
them; I have consumed them with the fire of my wrath:
their own way have I recompensed upon their heads,
saith the Lord GOD" (Ezekiel 22:30-31).

I wrote the following before I told my co-author what I was up to. In addition to bragging a bit on my Pastor, I wanted to provide a practical method to implement a trust in God that can provide oversized impact on your ministry, your community, and your outreach for Christ. Please use this is a blueprint for action in your own community.

On February 13, 2016, Associate Justice of the Supreme Court Antonin Scalia passed away in his sleep. The unexpected death of this stalwart jurist threw the future of the Court into question. In some ways, the ultimate direction of our country depended on how things would transpire over the next days, weeks, and months.

Pastor Brad Wells and GraceWay Baptist Church recognized the need for prayer in this situation and met that weekend on the steps of the Supreme

Court to pray for our nation and our leaders – to pray for revival in our land. For over ten straight years on Saturday evening, Pastor Wells has led a body of believers in this form of worship on the Supreme Court steps.

It was an action of obedience to make up the hedge and stand in the gap for our land. Fortunately, in this case, unlike the situation in Ezekiel 22, God found someone obedient to answer His call. And as this church body prays on the steps of the Supreme Court this Saturday evening yet again, may Christians all around this great nation be encouraged by their faithfulness and convicted of our own need in our own context to faithfully pray.

 "I exhort therefore, that, first of all, supplications, prayers, intercessions, and giving of thanks, be made for all men; For kings, and for all that are in authority; that we may lead a quiet and peaceable life in all godliness and honesty. For this is good and acceptable in the sight of God our Saviour; Who will have all men to be saved and come unto the knowledge of the truth" (I Timothy 2:1-4).

At face value there is nothing particularly powerful about prayers at such a location, yet this concept does provide a potent example of the presence of the Lord that pervades all institutions in our society. And, while a Saturday evening prayer time at the center of the power structures in Washington, D.C. doesn't exactly translate into standing before kings, it does provide an opportunity to call down God's influence on the buildings where major decisions are made that disproportionately influence our well-being.

Prayer at the major institutions of our society also provides both a personal and a public reminder that we refuse to cede any ground to the adversary. In fact, just the opposite – we are claiming God's promises that He can turn the heart of the king whithersoever He will (Proverbs 21:1). And such prayer provides an opportunity to sprinkle salt in places that need savor and shine light in places that need illumination (Matthew 5:13-16). It isn't an empty pharisaical show, but instead a full testimony that God's power is everywhere and God's people are unbowed to the cultural deities that clamor for our affection and allegiance.

I sincerely hope that the description above of what we call Supreme Prayer has not just been an exercise in observation. The intent has been to make it an exercise in replication and multiplication!

All Christians have a responsibility to be salt and light in our spheres of influence and realms of impact. We have been given the recipe for national revival in II Chronicles 7:14, and we need His people to start following it today. Unless you live in Washington D.C., you don't have a weekly prayer venue of the Supreme Court. Yet. each of us has an institution of significance in our own community – a city hall, a county courthouse, a school, or a public library. Christians can meet at such places with a group of like-minded believers to pray weekly for our nation, our community, and our leaders.

How can someone implement Supreme Prayer?

1. Set a regular time to meet at an institution of significance in your community.

2. Start your time together with a few songs of the faith.

3. Solicit prayer requests from those who have joined you about our nation, your community, and your church – have someone pray for these as a group.

4. Break up into smaller groups for follow-up prayer.

All the while, be sensitive to those who may be watching who could use an invitation to church, an explanation of what is happening, or a presentation of the gospel.

It is a way for all of us to make up the hedge and stand in the gap. Use this concept as an exercise of replication and multiplication in your own community to help prompt a revival that can spread throughout our land.

CHAPTER 21

NO!

BY JOHN TEICHERT

Several years ago, my family and I were driving down the highway listening to Christian hymns and singing along. At some point on this road trip, we heard a loud NO from the backseat. Assuming it was a standard sibling spat, we ignored it. A short while later, we heard the same thing. This time, we turned around to investigate. Seeing nothing out of the ordinary, we ignored it again. The third NO finally demanded parental action. We turned to our oldest daughter Summer, then five years old, and asked what was bothering her. She responded that it was the song's fault – an interesting answer.

The song included the following lyrics, rich with powerful spiritual truth:

It's out of your hands, you've done all you can do.
You've given God the problem, it's no longer up to you.
You've prayed the prayer of faith, now you're standing on God's truth.
While you're waiting on an answer, He has a question for you.

Is anything too hard for God?
Who's got a problem beyond His pow'r to solve?
Are there situations He's not the Master of?
Is anything too hard for God?

Only believe, trust His word, you'll see
That His plans are now unfolding, performing perfectly.
It's clear how much He loves you, just look at all He's done.
For all your questions, there is really only One.

Is anything too hard for God?
Who's got a problem beyond His pow'r to solve?
Are there situations He's not the Master of?
Is anything too hard for God?

What was Summer's problem with such a meaningful song? Not understanding the nuances of language at that age, she was adamantly responding to the rhetorical question, *Is Anything Too Hard For God?* and defiantly answering NO!

She was right; nothing is too hard for God, and as Sojourner Truth reminded us through a similar rhetorical question, God is not dead! With this firm doctrinal truth in mind, nothing should prevent us from begging the Lord for intervention in our land and fully engaging in a spirit of trust. To a spirit of resignation that discounts the Lord's power to change our great nation, we should firmly say NO!

SECTION 5

THE SCAM OF SEPARATION AND THE NOISE ABOUT NATIONALISM

"Commit thy works unto the LORD, and thy thoughts shall be established" (Proverbs 16:3).

"O my God, incline thine ear, and hear; open thine eyes, and behold our desolations, and the city which is called by thy name: for we do not present our supplications before thee for our righteousnesses, but for thy great mercies" (Daniel 9:18).

Our society is in an endless, fully-engaged political cycle. From certain factions, we hear ubiquitous calls for separation of church and state, and frequent claims decrying Christian Nationalism. All of it seems to be shaped by expedient political posturing, without careful thought about history, theology, or philosophy. In order to properly and wisely respond, it is critical to establish a firm understanding about a right view of America, American history, and Biblical Christianity to put everything written thus far into its proper context.

CHAPTER 22

GOD'S SIDE

BY JOHN TEICHERT

"But God forbid that I should glory, save in the cross of
our Lord Jesus Christ, by whom the world is crucified
unto me, and I unto the world" (Galatians 6:14).

We regularly see our politicians at all levels say anything and everything to gain a competitive advantage. Many invoke the name of the Lord, while striving to convince us that we should support them because God does. Whenever we hear such things, we must hearken back to the story about President Abraham Lincoln's that I shared in a previous chapter.

In the midst of that conflict, a minister urgently proclaimed that he "hoped the Lord was on our side." Lincoln thoughtfully and reverently responded: "I know that the Lord is always on the side of the right. But God is my witness that it is my constant anxiety and prayer, that both myself and this nation should be on the Lord's side."

In our lives, we must spend far less time assuming that God is on our side, and far more time ensuring that we are on His side. We are to avoid the presumptuous activities that seek to bend His will to match ours. We must not assume His alignment but instead assure our alignment.

Whenever we hear a political figure coax us with their faith-filled phrases, we must use the Lincoln litmus test. The question we should always ask ourselves is: Are we on His side? By the actions of our leaders, are they on His side? By their character, are they on His side? By their words, are they on His side? By their platforms, are they on His side? By their policies, are they on His side? By their track records, are they on His side? By their attitudes, are they on His side?

The statue of Reverend Billy Graham in the U.S. Capitol is informative in this respect. The Bible in the hands of Graham's statue is intentionally opened to Galatians 6:14. God forbid that Americans and our leaders glory in ourselves. Instead, may we all glory in a God who deserves our dedicated alignment.

There is one question we should always ask ourselves – are we on His side? Anything else is a subtle subversion of faith and a sneaky subordination of God. It is a stark sign of Christian Nationalism that makes the creation more important than the Creator.

OUR FOUNDING FATHER

"For who maketh thee to differ from another? And what hast thou that thou didst not receive? Now if thou didst receive it, why dost thou glory, as if thou hadst not received it?" (I Corinthians 4:7)

This nation is remarkable and exceptional. Regardless of what some detractors may say about this City on a Hill, it has been a beacon of light in a world often characterized by darkness. Yet, I Corinthians 4:7 offers us two important intertwined warnings about nationalism and pride.

What we have, we have received. The gift of liberty and prosperity in the form of the United States of America has been given to us by God and through a long line of faithful citizens. Some provided a vision; some provided a sacrifice; some provided innovation; some provided generosity; some provided community; some provided charity; some provided leadership; and some provided service. Yet, all has been built upon a foundation and within a context only possible through the blessings of God. As our Founders properly demonstrated, may we never forget that we have received whatever we have.

Because we have received what we have, we should be humble and not prideful. Our glory should be directed to God through humble thanksgiving. It is the Lord that made us to differ from another. It is through His gifts that this land was made possible and prosperous. The moment we take credit is the moment that we rob God of His rightful glory.

None of this is to say that our nation is to exclude the voices or rights of any citizen who makes up the great melting pot of our society. Any views that fail to treat fellow human beings as image-bearers of God or that use and manipulate an understanding of the Lord for selfish ends are an anathema to our founding principles and our way of life. Yet at the same time, despite our shortcomings, we must not be ashamed of who we are, where we came from, or the source of our hope for the future.

I am filled with pride in this great land, but such pride needs to be properly funneled towards the One who deserves the real credit. After all, He is our real Founding Father! And please don't trust me in this claim. Instead listen to an outside observer from France who saw something unique and special in this land.

CHAPTER 23

A PARTICULAR STRENGTH

BY JOHN TEICHERT

Alexis de Tocqueville, the French historian and political philosopher, marveled at the nation he observed first-hand in the middle of the 19th century. He saw the United States as a land characterized by Christianity and citizenship, duty and devotion, freedom and forward-thinking. It was a nation that had uniquely combined Christian principles into its core fabric and was prospering as a result.

As described in *Democracy in America*, de Tocqueville saw the "triumph of an idea" in action.

> *Christianity has therefore maintained a strong sway over the American mind and – something I wish to note above all – it rules not only like a philosophy taken up after evaluation but like a religion believed without discussion.*

> *It is religion which has given birth to Anglo-American societies: one must never lose sight of that; in the United States, religion is thus intimately linked to all national habits and all the emotions which one's native country arouses; that gives it a particular strength.*

Christianity of days past in America was treated with conviction and not just as a waning cultural artifact. As a result, it impacted the national spirit. It produced a harmonious, helpful, and happy society that wasn't perfect, but was intent on marching towards an alignment between its values and the application of those values.

"Master, which is the great commandment in the law? Jesus said unto him, Thou shalt love the Lord thy God with all thy heart, and with all thy soul, and with all thy mind. This is the first and great commandment. And the second is like unto it, Thou shalt love thy neighbor as thyself. On these two commandments hang all the law and the prophets" (Matthew 22:36-40).

Alexis de Tocqueville recognized America as a unique nation that had placed these Biblical priorities into action. Nineteenth-century Americans were motived by their love of God and a love of others. They used their freedoms to develop community not contention. They used their freedoms to extend a hand of help instead of grasping for personal excess. They used their freedoms to build institutions instead of destroying them.

> *In the United States, therefore, it was never intended for a man in a free country to have the right to do anything he liked; rather, social duties were imposed upon him more various than anywhere else.*
>
> *I must say that I have seen Americans making great and sincere sacrifices for the common good and a hundred times I have noticed that, when needs be, they almost always gave each other faithful support.*

The America so admired by de Tocqueville was the product of Christian principles that guided priorities away from selfishness and towards the Supreme and society. These priorities manifested themselves in a nation that was a model for others to follow.

"Therefore whosoever heareth these sayings of mine, and doeth them, I will liken him unto a wise man, which built his house upon a rock: And the rain descended, and the floods came, and the winds blew, and beat upon that house; and it fell not: for it was founded upon a rock" (Matthew 7:24-25).

Over a decade ago, Russian President Vladimir Putin made news by publishing an op-ed in *The New York Times*. In the midst of an opinion piece oozing with hypocrisy, Putin made an assertion not supported by history – America is unexceptional. Some inside and outside our country have claimed the same thing. Alexis de Tocqueville would disagree:

> *I have expressed enough to characterize Anglo-American civilization in its true colors. This civilization is the result (and this is something we must always bear in mind) of two quite distinct ingredients which anywhere else have often ended in war, but which Americans have succeeded somehow to meld together in wondrous harmony; namely the spirit of religion and the spirit of liberty.*

While de Tocqueville saw these concepts at cross-purposes in his European homeland, he saw them "intimately linked together in joint reign over the same land" in America. To him, this harmony and the land that enjoyed it was truly exceptional.

Importantly, the source of our exceptionalism is more fundamental than even these concepts. It comes from two foundations; one built upon another. The first is the foundation of the universe, the Lord Himself. We can be exceptional as a nation only as much as we are determined to reflect Him as individual citizens and as a society. The second is the foundation of the nation, the U.S. Constitution. When the Constitutional Convention ended on September 17, 1787, the Founding Fathers had created a foundational document that enshrined Biblical principles and translated them into a governmental structure. These two foundations are exceptional and inextricably linked, yielding an exceptional result.

"Who is the ultimate sovereign, God or man?" Rabbi Jonathan Sacks wisely asked. The uniqueness of the American Revolution did something unique in human history by recognizing the sovereignty of God as the source of societal rights and responsibilities. Yet, Sacks provided an important warning for us today that can erode our exceptionalism: "When human beings arrogate supreme power to themselves, politics loses its soul securing the defense of freedom." As we rob God of His sovereignty, then we remove the cornerstone of our exceptional foundation.

Sadly then, Putin may be partially right for a reason that would be completely foreign to him. It's not that American exceptionalism is errant and dangerous. It is simply waning because we have drifted away from our remarkable foundations. As the wise man builds his house upon a steady foundation, so too would a wise and exceptional nation cling tightly to its bedrock. Anything else would be unexceptional, failing when the rains descend, and the floods come, and the winds blow.

 "Now the Lord is that spirit: and where the Spirit of the Lord is, there is liberty" (II Corinthians 3:17).

Alexis de Tocqueville was struck by the impact that Christianity had on 19th century America:

> *America is still the country in the world where the Christian religion has retained the greatest real power over people's souls and nothing shows better how useful and natural religion is to man, since the country where it exerts the greatest sway is also the most enlightened and free.*

Our nation's Christian principles were unmistakable to the outside observer. In fact, such observation yielded one compelling conclusion – the great influence of Christianity had produced a remarkable nation.

CHAPTER 24

INSEPARABLE

BY BRAD WELLS

Standing before the Supreme Court of the United States, I listened to the guide explain the carving at the apex above the eastern entrance.

"Here we see one of our Founding Fathers holding a copy of the Constitution in one hand and the Bill of Rights in the other."

I stared intently at the carving of an elderly man with a full beard, dressed in long robes, and holding equally sized stone tablets on either side.

"Which Founding Father is he?" I asked knowingly.

"I'm not sure. Some say Thomas Jefferson or maybe John Adams," she replied.

It was obvious to me, and everyone in our group, the insignia represented Moses, the Great Lawgiver of 3,000 years past. He was seated in front holding two equally sized stone tablets in each hand with Confucius behind his right shoulder and the ancient Greek lawgiver Solon behind his left. The positioning not only suggested the prominence of the Law of God, but it also demanded all other wisdom submit to it.

This bold statement engraved in our nation's highest court demonstrates our Forefathers' strong conviction towards the Word of the eternal God.

Tragically, as our young guide shamelessly exhibited, a generation has arisen who can neither recognize our Founding Fathers, nor the Ten Commandments they revered.

Moses also looks down at the House of Representatives, directly in the face of the Speaker of the House, as he guides the legislative process. Our Founding Fathers recognized two important premises along these lines: 1) *morality,* not philosophy, is the basis for all human government, and 2) *we* are all moral agents.

Whenever we speak of morality, especially as delineated in the Ten Commandments, an outcry of "separation of church and state" arises. "'Right and wrong' are different for each person. We must allow the Constitution to rule the nation and moral creeds to rule individuals. Keep them separate," is the demand of secular society.

There are several problems with this demand. As this book has shown, our Founders never thought to separate God – who is the source of morality – from the state. Accordingly, this demand denies premise number 1. *Morality* is the basis of human government. Every form of government – from monarchy to democracy to tyranny – stands upon a foundational system of right and wrong. The difference is determined by the *what* and the *who.* What creed and Who said so?

Our Founding Fathers understood the corruptive tendencies of humanity and chose a system of transcendence, the Law of God. This choice required faith in the God of the Law as well. The two are inseparable.

They chose to agree with Moses when he said to the children of Israel, "For what nation is there so great, who hath God so nigh unto them, as the LORD our God is in all things that we call upon Him for? And what nation is there so great, that hath statutes and judgments so righteous as all this law, which I set before you this day?" (Deuteronomy 4:7-8).

Our Forefathers searched in vain to find a greater, more righteous system of government. They found God's form of government perfectly balanced in Isaiah 33:22, "For the LORD is our judge, the LORD is our lawgiver, the LORD is our king: He will save us." The distribution of judicial, legislative, and executive powers is the most stable foundation upon which to build a great nation.

Not only is all government built upon morality, but also premise number 2 declares *we* are moral agents.

Apostle Paul explains further that the law of God is written upon our *hearts*. "Which shew the work of the law written in their hearts, their conscience also bearing witness, and their thoughts the mean while accusing or else excusing one another" (Romans 2:15).

"Yes! As we said," replies secular humanism, "let your conscience be your guide."

The problem with human conscience, however, is it can lose its "true north." It can become impure, hardened, or "seared." Exposure to erroneous ideology and participation in evil deeds – with no repentance or redemption – will lead us far from the intention of the Creator.

"Now the Spirit speaketh expressly, that in the latter times some shall depart from the faith, giving heed to seducing spirits, and doctrines of devils; Speaking lies in hypocrisy; having their conscience seared with a hot iron" (1 Timothy 4:1-2).

There is constant debate about whether members of Congress should vote as the majority of their constituents would have them vote, or if they should vote as their own conscience would dictate.

The answer to this debate, in my opinion, is to be honest about who you are to your constituents and recalibrate daily to the Word of God. Remember, "Promotion cometh neither from the east, nor from the west, nor from the south. But God is the judge: He putteth down one, and setters up another" (Psalm 75:6-7).

If we are moral agents of a moral creed, we cannot separate our faith from our form, for it is indeed our *very foundation*.

Our forefathers may have borrowed from Greek, Roman, and Chinese philosophy; but as the carving over the Supreme Court entrance illustrates, every thought of man must filter through the eternal moral code, the very Word of God. It alone will stand the test of time and eternity.

In God We Trust is not debatable. It is *inseparable* from our very existence.

CHAPTER 25

THE SANCTION OF OUR EXAMPLE

BY JOHN TEICHERT

"The LORD bringeth the counsel of the heathen to nought: he maketh the devices of the people of none effect. The counsel of the LORD standeth for ever, the thoughts of his heart to all generations. Blessed is the nation whose God is the LORD; and the people whom he hath chosen for his own inheritance"
(Psalm 33:10-12).

On January 1, 1802, President Jefferson responded to the Danbury Baptists, creating the popularly known and misunderstood phrase *separation of church and state.* Over time, his words have been taken far out of context, distantly deviating and drastically diverging from the constitutional direction that "Congress shall make no law respecting an establishment of religion, or prohibiting the free exercise thereof." Jefferson and the Founders never intended for religious influence to be absent from governmental endeavors nor excluded from it. In fact, just the opposite.

Maybe the strongest proof of Jefferson's intent is what he did two days after writing that oft-twisted phrase. He went to church – in the U.S.

Capitol. Shortly after the Capitol opened its doors in 1800, the House of Representatives was used as the venue for Christian worship services every Sunday, and Jefferson was a regular parishioner. He had no problem with the People's House being used as a House of Worship.

Jefferson's actions following his letter to the Danbury Baptists provide crystalizing context for a twisted element of American history. Like other examples from our Founders, it is incompatible with the modern notion of the *separation of church and state* :

- The drafting of our first national seal by Jefferson and Franklin that reminded our fledgling nation of the need to follow God out of tyranny and towards liberty (p. 23).

- Our nation's first inauguration under the Constitution included:

  - The addition of "So Help Me God" by President Washington at the end of his oath of office (p. 80).

  - An inaugural speech that was far more of a sermon than it was a traditional political discourse (p. 80)

  - A Joint Resolution of Congress that mandated the new government attend a Christian worship service to praise God and pray for the new nation (p. 83–84).

- The same day that Congress passed the proposed Bill of Rights, including the First Amendment to the U.S. Constitution that enshrined religious liberty as our nation's first freedom, they also eagerly proposed a Joint Resolution calling for nationwide thanksgiving to the Lord (p. 71–72).

None of this is to say that we are a theocracy. The Constitution clearly prescribes that the federal government is to "make no law respecting an establishment of religion." Yet, our Founders demonstrated that there is no restriction in infusing our faith into our engagement with government. In fact, it would be foreign to them that we would limit ourselves from doing so.

As American Christian citizens today, may we be undeterred by those who would shout down our civic engagement by bombastic claims of *Christian Nationalism* or violations of *Separation of Church and State*. Instead, may we eagerly engage through the sanction of our example.

INTEGRITY FIRST

One of the most common mentorship questions I have received over the years is related to how to appropriately live out faith in the workplace – most often related to the military environment. The answer is long and multi-faceted, but one of the most powerful components of the answer is related to the first of the three core values of the United States Air Force – Integrity First.

Our military service calls on its 700,000 members to live with integrity – consistently and steadfastly.

There are two primary components of integrity – the first is honesty. If I were to live my life in a work setting by scrubbing out the bedrock components upon which my character rests that are driven by my Christian faith, then I would be living a fundamentally dishonest existence. I would be hiding the core component of a worldview that shapes my perspective and molds my life. Thus, I must not hide my faith or I would be violating Integrity First.

The second component of integrity is wholeness. It is living an undivided existence in which I align the entirety of my life – my words, thoughts, and actions – with my values, morals, and principles. Integrity means not separating your life into components but living a whole life in which all parts fit together into one complete entity. If I were to hide the faith component of my life at work, then I would artificially divide a character and personality that are meant to be indivisible. As a result, I would be violating Integrity First.

The concepts are simple. If you hide your faith in the workplace, then you are finding two ways to violate the first core value of our organization. This isn't to say that you go out of your way to inappropriately create a distraction that diverts the focus of the workplace from its mission and purpose. But, it is comforting that secular organizational core values insist that we don't hide a core element of who we are and Whose we are!

CHAPTER 26

OUR PRACTICES AND OUR PRINCIPLES

BY JOHN TEICHERT

I was recently asked about my reasons for hope for our country and our society in a secular context. I'm an upbeat and optimistic personality, and my kids sometimes call me *extra*. I don't think it is always a compliment.

I often reflect on the life and words of a hero of mine to describe my optimism – escaped slave Frederick Douglass whom I wrote about previously. Douglass stated the following hard truth in 1852 when asked to give remarks on Independence Day in a speech entitled "What to the Slave Is the Fourth of July":

> *This Fourth [of] July is yours, not mine. You may rejoice, I must mourn. To drag a man in fetters into the grand illuminated temple of liberty, and call upon him to join you in joyous anthems, were inhuman mockery and sacrilegious irony. Do you mean, citizens, to mock me, by asking me to speak to-day?*

Following these strongly condemning words, Douglass went on to say the following:

> *The American people, likewise, have made void their law by their traditions; they have trampled upon their own constitution, stepped beyond the limits set for themselves, and, in their ever-abounding iniquity, established a constitution of action outside of the fundamental law of the land. While the one is good, the other is evil; while the one is for liberty, the other is in favour of slavery; the practice of the American government is one thing, and the character of the constitution of the government is quite another and different thing.*

There is an important nuance here that follows the thoughts of the Preamble to the U.S. Constitution: we are in the midst of forming "a more perfect union." That means that we are not yet perfect and while we are progressing in a non-steady fashion, we are committed to stiving to align ourselves with our founding principles. As Douglass reminds us, it isn't a *principle* problem but an *application* problem.

With the scars of whip marks on his back, Douglass went on in his remarks to describe the Constitution as "a GLORIOUS LIBERTY DOCUMENT" (emphasis provided by Douglass). He went on to explain that our Founders were "great men" and "brave men." He stated that those founding fathers "are entitled to the profound gratitude of mankind."

Our Founders weren't perfect. Our history isn't perfect. We are not perfect! But it is not because our principles are flawed. It is because we have not yet aligned our practices with our GLORIOUS LIBERTY principles. A constant pursuit of those principles should motivate our every action and inform our daily perspective as we struggle for a *more perfect union.*

CONCLUSION

CHAPTER 27

HIS TABERNACLE

BY BRAD WELLS

stepped off the plane to see my name printed on a placard held high above the crowd. The airport concierge smiled broadly with acknowledgment, gathered my luggage, and whisked me deftly through customs. Having traveled abroad countless times, the honor of walking past the weary lines of tourists was nothing less than exhilarating. In no time, I found myself seated comfortably in a black shuttle bus, weaving my way through the streets of a foreign land.

I had arrived, along with several others, for the purpose of negotiating peace. We were a delegation from varied backgrounds called upon to speak on behalf of those we represented. In my case, I represented conservative churches in my particular denomination.

There were other representations in our delegation; all religious, but not all spiritually discernible. The pretense and posturing were palpable. One gentleman thanked the rest of us for joining "his team." I had never met him before and had no idea he would be part of the delegation. A woman spoke forcefully of the "work" she had done to get to this place. None of the others knew of it. Another delegate never showed up. His ticket had been purchased, his hotel reserved; yet he never appeared.

It became immediately apparent that our western mindset was very different than the one with which we were negotiating. While we were impressed with power and position, they were driven by pride and shame. While we jockeyed for prominence within the delegation, they watched for our authentic insight into their situation.

The question at hand was that of land ownership. I had one word for the rightful owner: Occupy.

To occupy means to take control of a place, to live or reside in it, to fill it up, and to keep your attention upon it.

It begins with planting a garden, which grows into a sustainable farm. Once it is "fit in the field," a home can be built nearby (Proverbs 24:27).

Others will join, creating a settlement, and eventually organizing into a community.

Then, support to defend the occupation can amass. Defense must have three-legged stability: spiritual, intellectual, and physical.

Establish worship and commit to obeying the Creator of the land.

Educate each person equally, providing strong minds an understanding of their existence.

Lastly, protect the borders of your occupation.

To prove the wisdom of the wisest man who ever lived, the Bible presents the scenario of two women fighting over one baby. Standing before the king's court to settle the dispute, the women argue and squabble, each pulling at one child, nearly tearing it in two.

The king raises his hand and shouts above the confusion, "Bring me a sword! Let us divide the child and give half to one and half to the other" (I Kings 3:24-25).

One woman readily agrees, "Yes, let it be neither mine nor yours!"

The other cries out, "No! Do not harm the child. Let her have it and in no wise slay it!"

The king wisely discerns the rightful mother is the one who cares for the child itself, not the one who only wishes to claim ownership no matter if it lives or dies.

Let me repeat, the rightful owner is the one who will sacrifice to care for the child. If you own the land, *occupy* it. Declare ownership. Care for it. Defend it.

The king will give you the whole baby if it truly belongs to you.

I was asked for counsel in a debate over which I hold little sway and for which I will lose little.

But the story of the land struggle is a metaphor for all of humanity. It goes like this:

We are the land. The enemy of our souls would claim ownership over *us*. He lords over our base natures, wresting control as we yield to sin. He promises peace and prosperity; but his real plan is to steal our joy, kill our hope, and destroy our future. He will occupy every part of us, if we allow him a quarter in any part.

"There is no peace, saith my God, to the wicked" (Isaiah 57:21). Turmoil, fear, and death lay in the wake of those who would surrender to the enemy and follow his demands.

But there is another standing with nail-pierced hands, bearing the wounds of rightful ownership. "For He is our peace," Ephesians 2:14 says. He gave His own body on the tree to pay for our sin and reconcile us to God.

This One can be trusted. He owns the land and everything in it. He has a plan for peace written in His own blood. Will we not yield to His control and find peace *with God*?

The second point of His peace plan can be found in the next verse, "He ... hath broken down the middle wall of partition between us ... so making peace" (Ephesians 2:15). Not only does the Prince of Peace want us to have peace *with Him*, He desires we have peace *with one another*.

The division in the delegation mentioned above was rooted in the desire to *own the room* as we each presented our peace plan. We were tripping over all the names dropped on the floor, vying for sway over the outcome.

Apostle Paul has one question for just such a scenario, "Is Christ divided?" (I Corinthians 1:13).

There is no situation in our family, our community, our workplace, or our church that He does not want to *occupy*. Shall I define that word again? Control. Reside. Fill. Keep.

"That in all things He might have the preeminence" (Colossians 1:18).

"Only by pride cometh contention," also a quote by the wisest man (Proverbs 13:10).

When we experience strife and contention in relationships, pride has taken up residence. We have allowed a "squatter" on land which belongs to the Prince of Peace. Soon after pride breaks ground, uncleanness and impurity of every sort will spring up. "For where envying and strife is, there is confusion and every evil work" (James 3:16).

Is there a part of your relationship with others that is not under the control of your Creator? Is there a conversation in which He would not be welcome? Is there division over who gets recognition and promotion? If so, expect a rotten harvest and an enemy occupation.

Let go! Turn over ownership of negotiations to the God of promotion. If you will humble yourself, He will exalt you in due time.

Digging deeper in the soil of struggle, we find the real root of "wars and fightings among you" comes from *our hearts* (James 4:1). Divisions without flow from the division within.

We have our carefully crafted masks, projecting what we *want* others to think we are. We conceal and hide behind paranoia, hoping against hope we are convincing enough.

But we can't hide our reputation. This is what others *really* think we are. It comes from an objective point of view—well, at least as objective as *their* lens and prejudice.

Of course, we identify as we *think* we are, our ego and self-image readily agreeing with us.

Then, there's the truth: who we *really* are. Our character, nothing more and nothing less.

Oh, what a maze of turmoil self-awareness is!

Who are we? We are an eternal soul, placed in a body and culture to reveal what we think, what we feel, and what we want. And each choice has an eternal consequence.

Fellow Christ-follower, let us get one thing straight: we are *not* the owner!

"What? know ye not that your body is the temple of the Holy Ghost which is in you, which ye have of God, and ye are not your own? For ye are bought with a price: therefore glorify God in your body, and in your spirit, which are God's" (I Corinthians 6:19-20).

Why is ownership of our body so important to God? Because, just as He dwelt in a physical tabernacle under the old covenant, He desires to dwell in our *physical bodies* under the new covenant. In fact, He has delegated no other place in which to exhibit His glory than through our physical bodies joining collectively into the Body of Christ – the Church!

"Know ye not that ye are the temple of God, and that the Spirit of God dwelleth in you? If any man defile the temple of God, him shall God destroy; for the temple of God is holy, which temple ye are" (I Corinthians 3:16-17).

When I trust in God, I become the holy tabernacle of His dwelling.

It is true Ephesians 3:21 says, "Unto Him be glory in the church." Yet, the church of Jesus Christ is made up of *individual* Christians who are filled with the Holy Spirit of God. Words fail me to express the magnitude of this privilege!

As Christians who have made peace *with God,* we can now live in the peace *of God* every day of our short existence on this earth.

"Be careful for nothing; but in every thing by prayer and supplication with thanksgiving let your requests be made known unto God. And *the peace of God*, which passeth all understanding, shall keep your hearts and minds through Christ Jesus" (Philippians 4:6-7).

It is only a matter of full surrender to the rightful owner. *All* is to be given over to the occupation of the Prince of Peace. The One who sacrificed for us has every right to every part of us. He must control, reside, fill, and keep our hearts and minds through Christ Jesus!

When I trust in God, I am at peace with God, with those around me, and with myself.

When I trust in God, I become His tabernacle.

CHAPTER 28

A LONG ROAD AND A GREAT DESIRE

BY JOHN TEICHERT

"Pray without ceasing" (I Thessalonians 5:17).

"Rejoicing in hope; patient in tribulation; continuing instant in prayer" (Romans 12:12).

By the evening of June 6, 1944, the invasion of mainland Europe had seen an amazing first day of activity. Over 150,000 Allied troops had landed on French soil, transported by thousands of aircraft and ships in a massive surprise military operation. President Roosevelt spoke to the nation that evening, but more importantly, he led the nation in prayer. In part, he shared the following that can be seen as a perfect charge for us today:

Almighty God: Our sons, pride of our Nation, this day have set upon a mighty endeavor, a struggle to preserve our Republic, our religion, and our civilization, and to set free a suffering humanity.

Lead them straight and true; give strength to their arms, stoutness to their hearts, steadfastness in their faith.

They will need Thy blessings. Their road will be long and hard. For the enemy is strong. He may hurl back our forces. Success may not come with rushing speed, but we shall return again and again; and we know that by Thy grace, and by the righteousness of our cause, our sons will triumph.

They will be sore tried, by night and by day, without rest-until the victory is won. The darkness will be rent by noise and flame. Men's souls will be shaken with the violences of war.

For these men are lately drawn from the ways of peace. They fight not for the lust of conquest. They fight to end conquest. They fight to liberate. They fight to let justice arise, and tolerance and good will among all Thy people. They yearn but for the end of battle, for their return to the haven of home.

Some will never return. Embrace these, Father, and receive them, Thy heroic servants, into Thy kingdom.

And for us at home – fathers, mothers, children, wives, sisters, and brothers of brave men overseas – whose thoughts and prayers are ever with them – help us, Almighty God, to rededicate ourselves in renewed faith in Thee in this hour of great sacrifice.

Many people have urged that I call the Nation into a single day of special prayer. But because the road is long and the desire is great, I ask that our people devote themselves in a continuance of prayer. As we rise to each new day, and again when each day is spent, let words of prayer be on our lips, invoking Thy help to our efforts.

Give us strength, too – strength in our daily tasks, to redouble the contributions we make in the physical and the material support of our armed forces.

And let our hearts be stout, to wait out the long travail, to bear sorrows that may come, to impart our courage unto our sons wheresoever they may be.

And, O Lord, give us Faith. Give us Faith in Thee; Faith in our sons; Faith in each other; Faith in our united crusade. Let not the keenness of our spirit ever be dulled. Let not the impacts of temporary events, of temporal matters of but fleeting moment – let not these deter us in our unconquerable purpose.

With Thy blessing, we shall prevail over the unholy forces of our enemy. Help us to conquer the apostles of greed and racial arrogancies. Lead us to the saving of our country, and with our sister Nations into a world unity that will spell a sure peace – a peace invulnerable to the schemings of unworthy men. And a peace that will let all of men live in freedom, reaping the just rewards of their honest toil.

Thy will be done, Almighty God. Amen.

President Roosevelt's charge wasn't for a one-time prayer or a one-day prayer, but a prayer without ceasing. The American people were to "devote themselves in a continuance of prayer." Our predecessors were called to rededicate themselves through renewed faith and trust at a time of highest consequence.

As we reflect upon that desperate hour over eight decades ago, we must do the same today. Let words of trusting prayer for this nation be constantly on our lips.

SERVICE

Nathan Hale volunteered to be a patriot spy for General Washington behind enemy lines in New York City in September 1776. The 21-year-old graduate of Yale was determined to "reflect and do nothing but what duty demands."

Yet, following an aggressive purging campaign during the great fire in lower Manhattan, the British apprehended Hale and sentenced him to death as a spy. The next day, on September 22, Hale was led to an artillery park near General Howe's headquarters to face the noose.

As a part of Hale's last words, he gave a "sensible and spirited speech." Then, with the promise of a long life ahead extinguished, Hale shared the following famous words: "I only regret that I have but one life to lose for my country." Upon that phrase, he was executed.

Hale wasn't originally sure that military service was right for him. He had signed a teaching contract before the Revolutionary War began and was conflicted as to whether he should break that contract to fight for the cause of freedom. He received the following advice from a dear friend: "Was I in your condition, I think the more extensive service would be my choice. Our holy Religion, the honor of our God, a glorious country, and a happy constitution is what we have to defend." Hale took this advice to heart and selected the more extensive service.

What happened to Christians in this nation who would select the more extensive service? Instead of defending our holy religion, the honor of our God, our glorious country, and our happy constitution, we relent to lesser pursuits. We decide to invest our time, our attention, our energy, our talents, and our resources in things that are far less important and far less noble. All the while, our opponents are fully invested in diminishing the things that we hold dear.

In what would be a familiar theme to Nathan Hale, Sir Francis Drake penned the following in 1579:

Disturb us, Lord, when
We are too well pleased with ourselves,
When our dreams have come true
Because we have dreamed too little,
When we arrived safely
Because we sailed too close to the shore.

Disturb us, Lord, when
With the abundance of things we possess
We have lost our thirst
For the waters of life;
Having fallen in love with life,
We have ceased to dream of eternity
And in our efforts to build a new earth,
We have allowed our vision
Of the new Heaven to dim.

Disturb us, Lord, to dare more boldly,
To venture on wider seas
Where storms will show your mastery;
Where losing sight of land,
We shall find the stars.

We ask You to push back
The horizons of our hopes;
And to push into the future
In strength, courage, hope and love.
This we ask in the name of our Captain,
Who is Jesus Christ.

What a series of stunning thoughts. By faith and trust, we must thirst for the waters of life, to dream of eternity, to expand our vision of heaven, to dare more boldly, to venture on to wider seas, to expand our horizons of hope, and to push into the future with strength, courage, hope and love.

Like Hale, today we must choose the more extensive service! And as Drake reminds us, we must be willing to lose sight of land to find the stars!

TIS WELL

President Washington passed into eternity on December 14, 1799. He had gotten sick from riding his horse on a cold and rainy day on his Mount Vernon estate.

Among his final words, Washington resolutely proclaimed: "I am not afraid to go," and he closed his life with the final phrase "Tis Well." He was able to speak so boldly because he understood the words from The Book of John which he had inscribed on his tomb:

"I am the resurrection and the life, saith the Lord, he that believeth in me, though he were dead, yet shall he live; and whosoever liveth and believeth in me shall never die." (John 11:25-26).

It is through his trust in this eternity-shaking truth that Washington gained boldness – in life and in death.

It is easy to lament the situation in which we find ourselves in this challenging age. But, how do we have perfect peace as we navigate the challenges we face? The prophet Isaiah tells us: "Thou wilt keep him in perfect peace, whose mind is stayed on thee: because he trusteth in thee. Trust ye in the LORD for ever: for in the LORD JEHOVAH is everlasting strength" (Isaiah 26:3-4).

No matter the situation, may we live and die with Washington's trust-filled words on our lips and in our hearts – Tis Well!

ENDNOTES

Introduction – Enshrined

Pg 1. *On March 3rd, 1865*: "H. Rept. 112-47," Congress.gov, https://www.congress.gov/committee-report/112th-congress/house-report/47/1

Pg 3. *In God Alone Is Our Trust*: "In God We Trust: Abraham Lincoln and America's Deathbed Repentance," Justin Latterell, *Political Theology*, April 21, 2015.

Chapter 2 – Teichert's Take on Trust

Pg 19. *We need Thy strength*: "For God's Grace in Our Helplessness," *The Prayers of Peter Marshall*, Ed. Catherine Marshall, 1949, p. 97.

Pg 19. *At this moment*: "Presidential Speeches: Harry S. Truman Presidency: April 16, 1945: First Speech to Congress," UVA Miller Center, https://millercenter.org/the-presidency/presidential-speeches/april-16-1945-first-speech-congress.

Pg 19. *Truman had but a fraction*: *The Accidental President: Harry S. Truman and the Four Months That Changed the World*, A. J. Baime, 2018, p. 136.

Pg 19–20. *The first four months*: Ibid, p. ix.

Pg 20. *35,000 decisions a day*: "A Simple Way to Make Better Decisions," Amanda Reill, *Harvard Business Review*, December 5, 2023.

Pg 23. *On July 4th, 1776*: "The Great Seal," *National Museum of American Diplomacy*, March 19, 2018, https://diplomacy.state.gov/the-great-seal/. Also in *The Papers of John Adams*, Ed. Robert J. Taylor, 1977.

Pg 23. *Yet, their drafts powerfully reveal:* "John Adams to Abigail Adams, 14 August 1776," https://founders.archives.gov/documents/Adams/04-02-02-0059.

Chapter 3 – Building on a Clean Foundation

Pg 29. *most important duty to God: Humility: The Journey Toward Holiness,* Andrew Murray, 1895, Chp 12.

Chapter 4 – The Faithful Foundations of a New Nation

Pg 34. *Gravity explains the motions:* https://www.goodreads.com/author/quotes/135106.Isaac_Newton. I have not independently verified this quote.

Pg 34. *I find more remarks of authenticity: An Apology for Christianity,* Richard Watson, 1776.

Pg 34. *Atheism is so senseless:* https://www.goodreads.com/quotes/7952880-opposite-to-godliness-is-atheism-in-profession-and-idolatry-in. I have not independently verified this quote.

Pg 34. *He who thinks half-heartedly:* https://www.goodreads.com/author/quotes/135106.Isaac_Newton. I have not independently verified this quote.

Pg 34. *Standing on the shoulders of giants:* "Isaac Newton letter to Robert Hooke, 1675," *Historical Society of Pennsylvania,* https://digitallibrary.hsp.org/index.php/Detail/objects/9792.

Pg 35. *When I left home:* "A Sermon on the Services and Death of Abraham Lincoln," Rev. John Falkner Blake, April 16, 1865, https://lincoln.digitalscholarship.emory.edu/blake-001/.

Pg 37. *Now I see that the Englishman's God: New England's Memorial,* Nathaniel Morton, 1669.

Pg 37. *We know, O Lord: The Power of Faith,* Woodi Ishmael, 1965, p. 82.

Pg 38. *The Revolution is the most important event in our history*: "Gordon S. Wood: How the American Revolution 'infused into our culture our noblest ideals and highest aspirations,'" Library of America, March 31, 2016, https://www.loa.org/news-and-views/639-gordon-s-wood-how-the-american-revolution-infused-into-our-culture-our-noblest-ideals-and-highest-aspirations/.

Pg 38. *I've spoken of the shining city all my political life*: "Farewell Address to the Nation," Ronald Reagan Presidential Library and Museum, January 11, 1989, https://www.reaganlibrary.gov/archives/speech/farewell-address-nation.

Pg 39. *For we must consider that we shall be as a City upon a hill*: "A Model of Christian Charity," Teaching American History, 1630, https://teachingamericanhistory.org/document/a-model-of-christian-charity-2/.

Pg 39. *The New England clergy*: *The New England Clergy and the American Revolution*, Alice M. Baldwin, 1928, p. xii.

Pg 40. *These and like sermons and pamphlets*: Ibid, p. 45.

Pg 40. *There is not a right asserted*: Ibid, p. 170.

Pg 41. *O Lord our Heavenly Father*: "First Prayer of the Continental Congress, 1774," Office of the Chaplain: United States House of Representatives, https://chaplain.house.gov/archive/continental.html.

Pg 42. *I never saw a greater Effect upon an Audience*: "John Adams to Abigail Adams, 16 September 1774, National Archives: Founders Online, https://founders.archives.gov/documents/Adams/04-01-02-0101.

Pg 42. *God would graciously pour out His Holy Spirit*: "History of Prayer in America," National Day of Prayer Task Force, https://www.nationaldayofprayer.org/about/history_of_prayer_in_america.

Pg 43. *consistent with a determined resolution and Christian firmness*: *The Battle of Lexington: A Sermon & Eyewitness Narrative*, Ed. Rev Christopher Hoops, 2007, (originally published in 1776), p. 39-40.

Pg 43. *But it is not by us alone that this day is to be noticed*: *The Battle of Lexington: A Sermon & Eyewitness Narrative*, Ed. Rev Christopher Hoops, 2007, (originally published in 1776), p. 45.

Pg 43. *the shot heard round the world*: "Concord Hymn," Ralph Waldo Emerson, 1837.

Pg 44. *The General most earnestly requires*: "General Orders, 4 July 1775," National Archives: Founders Online, https://founders.archives.gov/documents/Washington/03-01-02-0027.

Pg 45. *In the following pages*: *The Writings of Thomas Paine, Vol. 1* (1774-1779), Ed. Moncure Daniel Conway, 1894.

Pg 45. *But where say some is the King of America?*: Ibid.

Chapter 5 – The Spark That Ignited a Movement of Trust

Pg 47. *San Diego, California*: https://bigbayboom.com/news/videos-2012/.

Pg 48. *Is it not that, in the chain of human events*: "Speech on Independence Day, John Quincy Adams, July 4, 1837," Teaching American History, https://teachingamericanhistory.org/document/speech-on-independence-day-2/.

Pg 49. *Halifax Resolves*: "The Halifax Resolves," NCpedia, https://www.ncpedia.org/history/usrevolution/halifax-resolves.

Pg 49. *Resolved, That these United Colonies*: "Journals of the Continental Congress – Resolution of Richard Henry Lee; June 7, 1776," Yale Law School: The Avalon Project, Documents in Law, History, and Diplomacy, https://avalon.law.yale.edu/18th_century/contcong_06-07-76.asp.

Pg 53. *God who gave us life gave us liberty.*: The National Park Service: Thomas Jefferson Memorial, excerpted from multiple sources, https://www.nps.gov/thje/learn/photosmultimedia/quotations.htm.

Pg 53. *source of inspiration was the Hebrew Bible*: "The Universal Story," Jonathan Sacks: The Rabbi Sacks Legacy, 9 April 2010, https://rabbisacks.org/archive/the-universal-story/.

Pg 53. *the tree of liberty has religious roots*: "In Defence of Religious Liberty: Acceptance speech at the Becket Fund for Religious Liberty," Jonathan Sacks: The Rabbi Sacks Legacy, 15 May, 2014, https://rabbisacks.org/videos/defence-religious-liberty/.

Pg 53–54. *will be the most memorable Epocha*: "Letter from John Adams to Abigail Adams, 3 July 1776," Massachusetts Historical Society: Collections Online, https://www.masshist.org/database/viewer.php?item_id=102&pid=17.

Chapter 6 – At All Times Necessary

Pg 55. *The General hopes his important Event*: "General Orders, 9 July 1776," National Archives: Founders Online, https://founders.archives.gov/documents/Washington/03-05-02-0176.

Pg 56. *The Honorable Continental Congress*: Ibid.

Pg 57. *the blessing and protection of Heaven*: Ibid.

Pg 57. *heaven inspired*: "The United States Elevated to Glory and Honor," University of Nebraska – Lincoln: Electronic Texts in American Studies, 1783, https://digitalcommons.unl.edu/cgi/viewcontent.cgi?article=1041&context=etas.

Pg 57. *sealed and confirmed by God Almighty*: Ibid.

Pg 58. *My brave fellows*: "Washington encouraging his men to re-enlist in the Army: Tuesday, December 31, 1776," George Washington's Mount Vernon, https://www.mountvernon.org/library/digitalhistory/past-projects/quotes/article/my-brave-fellows-you-have-done-all-i-asked-you-to-do-and-more-than-can-be-reasonably-expected-but-your-country-is-at-stake-your-wives-your-houses-and-all-that-you-hold-dear-you-have-worn-yourselves-out-with-fatigues-and-hardships-but-we-know-not-how-to-sp.

Pg 58. *God Almighty inclined their hearts to listen*: *1776*, David McCullough, 2006, p. 286.

Pg 58–59. *The year 1776*: Ibid, p. 294.

Pg 59. *Upon my return from the army of Baltimore*: "Benjamin Rush to John Adams, 24 February 1790," National Archives: Founders Online, https://founders.archives.gov/documents/Adams/06-20-02-0154.

Pg 60–61. *FORASHMUCH as it is the indispensable Duty of all Men*: "In Congress. November 1, 1777," Library of Congress, https://tile.loc.gov/storage-services/service/rbc/rbpe/rbpe04/rbpe040/04001400/04001400.pdf.

Pg 61. *For without arrogance or the smallest deviation*: "George Washington to John Banister, 21 April 1778," National Archives: Founders Online, https://founders.archives.gov/documents/Washington/03-14-02-0525.

Pg 62. *One of the most inspiring portrayals of American history*: "Proclamation 5551 – Thanksgiving Day, 1986," Ronald Reagan Presidential Library & Museum, https://www.reaganlibrary.gov/archives/speech/proclamation-5551-thanksgiving-day-1986.

Pg 62. *Such a prayer I never heard*: "Washington in Prayer," UShistory.org: Historic Valley Forge, https://www.ushistory.org/valleyforge/washington/prayer.html?srsltid=AfmBOorFYtyWZDHpDV4T9v_5HH6TaVEQCDI63OnLKG7TD_p891cIM_Zz.

Pg 63. *Tomorrow being the day set apart by the Honorable Congress*: "General Orders, 17 December 1777," National Archives: Founders Online, https://founders.archives.gov/documents/Washington/03-12-02-0566.

Pg 64. *For in all the world's history*: *Washington: A Biography*, Benson Lossing, 1860.

Pg 65. *We have, as you very justly observe*: "George Washington to William Gordon, 9 March 1781," National Archives: Founders Online, https://founders.archives.gov/documents/Washington/03-31-02-0019.

Pg 65. *The man must be bad indeed who can look upon the events of the American Revolution*: "George Washington to Samuel Langdon, 28 September 1789," National Archives: Founders Online, https://founders.archives.gov/documents/Washington/05-04-02-0070.

Chapter 7 – The Work of a Divine Providence

Pg 68. *I do not believe that the Constitution was the offspring of inspiration*: "Benjamin Rush: Observations on the Fourth of July Procession in Philadelphia," *Pennsylvania Mercury*, 15 July 1788, https://archive.csac.history.wisc.edu/benjamin_rush7.15.88.pdf.

Pg 68. *In this situation of this Assembly*: "Benjamin Franklin: Constitutional Convention Address on Prayer," American Rhetoric: Online Speech Bank, https://www.americanrhetoric.com/speeches/benfranklin.htm.

Pg 69. *I have lived, Sir, a long time, and the longer I live*: Ibid.

Pg 70. *President Clinton today signed into law*: "Clinton Signs Law Protecting Religious Practices," *The New York Times*, Peter Steinfels, November 17, 1993, https://www.nytimes.com/1993/11/17/us/clinton-signs-law-protecting-religious-practices.html.

Pg 70. *The free exercise of religion has been called the first freedom*: "Remarks on Signing the Religious Freedom Restoration Act of 1993," The American Presidency Project, November 16, 1993, https://www.presidency.ucsb.edu/documents/remarks-signing-the-religious-freedom-restoration-act-1993.

Pg 70. *What this law basically says is that the Government*: Ibid.

Pg 70–71. *I'm told that, as many of the people in the coalition worked together*: Ibid.

Pg 71. *That a joint committee of both Houses be directed*: "United States Congress Proclamation (September 25, 1789)," American Minute, https://americanminute.com/blogs/american-quotations-by-william-j-federer-2024/united-states-congress-proclamation-september-25-1789. Also in *Joint Resolution of October 3, 1789, for a National Day of Thanksgiving*, United States Congress, 1789.

Pg 71. *It is the duty of all Nations*: "Thanksgiving Proclamation of 1789," George Washington's Mount Vernon, https://www.mountvernon.org/education/primary-source-collections/primary-source-collections/article/thanksgiving-proclamation-of-1789.

Pg 72. *It is impossible to consider the degree*: "James Madison to Thomas Jefferson, 24 October 1787," National Archives: Founders Online, https://founders.archives.gov/documents/Madison/01-10-02-0151.

Pg 72. *will demonstrate as visibly the finger of Providence*: "Divine Intervention in the Ratification Process," University of Wisconsin – Madison: Center for the Study of the American Constitution, https://csac.history.wisc.edu/document-collections/religion-and-the-ratification/divine-intervention/.

Pg 72. *For my own part, I sincerely esteem it a system*: "The Finger of God on the Constitutional Convention," Wall Builders, https://wallbuilders.com/resource/the-finger-of-god-on-the-constitutional-convention/.

Pg 72. *The constitutional convention and the written constitution*: *The New England Clergy and the American Revolution*, Alice M. Baldwin, 1928, p. 134.

Pg 72–73. *I believe no one can read the history of our country*: "Religion: Breakfast in Washington," *Time Magazine*, February 15, 1954, https://time.com/archive/6869292/religion-breakfast-in-washington/.

Pg 73. *I believe the entire Bill of Rights*: Ibid.

Pg 74. *The teachings of the Bible are so interwoven*: Library of Congress, https://crowd.loc.gov/campaigns/rough-rider-bull-moose-theodore-roosevelt/2-mar-7-sept-15-1901-vice-presidency-and-mckinleys-assassination/mss382990015/mss382990015-513/.

Pg 74–75. *The great difference between the maxims of the world*: *Value of the Bible and Excellence of the Christian Religion: For the Use of Families and Schools,* Noah Webster, 1834, p. 79.

Pg 75. *Almost all the civil liberty,* Ibid, p. 89-90.

Chapter 8 – A Sacred Cause and a Sacred Fire

Pg 77. *sacred cause:* "General Orders, 17 December 1777," National Archives: Founders Online, https://founders.archives.gov/documents/Washington/03-12-02-0566.

Pg 77. *sacred fire of liberty*: "President George Washington's First Inaugural Speech (1789)," National Archives: Milestone Documents, https://www.archives.gov/milestone-documents/president-george-washingtons-first-inaugural-speech.

Pg 77. *eternal rules of order and right*: Ibid.

Pg 78. *About 10 o'clock I bade adieu to Mount Vernon*: "April 1789," National Archives: Founders Online, https://founders.archives.gov/documents/Washington/01-05-02-0005-0001.

Pg 78. *Among the vicissitudes incident to life*: "President George Washington's First Inaugural Speech (1789)," National Archives: Milestone Documents, https://www.archives.gov/milestone-documents/president-george-washingtons-first-inaugural-speech.

Pg 79. *On the morning of the day on which your illustrious President*: "America's Religious Heritage As Demonstrated in Presidential Inaugurations," Wall Builders, https://wallbuilders.com/resource/americas-religious-heritage-as-demonstrated-in-presidential-inaugurations/#_edn5.

Pg 80. *Such being the impressions*: "President George Washington's First Inaugural Speech (1789)," National Archives: Milestone Documents, https://www.archives.gov/milestone-documents/president-george-washingtons-first-inaugural-speech.

Pg 81. *In tendering this homage to the Great Author*: Ibid.

Pg 82. *I dwell on this prospect with every satisfaction*: Ibid.

Pg 83. *Having thus imported to you my sentiments*: Ibid.

Pg 83. *Resolved, That, after the oath shall have been administered*: "Journal of the Senate of the United States, 1789," Congress.gov, https://www.congress.gov/senate-journal/19.

Pg 84. *The President, the Vice-President, the Senate, and the House of Representatives*: "The Debates and Proceedings in the Congress of the United States, First Congress, First Session, Volume 1," UNT Digital Libraries, https://digital.library.unt.edu/ark:/67531/metadc29465/m1/18/.

Pg 84. *Psalms, I Kings, Acts, and III John*: "America's Religious Heritage As Demonstrated in Presidential Inaugurations," Wall Builders, https://wallbuilders.com/resource/americas-religious-heritage-as-demonstrated-in-presidential-inaugurations/#_edn5.

Pg 84–85. *One of the really great heritages of the American people*: *Strength For Service to God and Country (Feb 3)*, Ed. Norman Nygaard, 1942.

Pg 85. *The American people, likewise*: *The Speeches of Frederick Douglass*, Ed. John r. McKivigan, Julie Husband, and Heather L. Kaufman, 2018, p. 164-5.

Pg 86. *the Constitution is a GLORIOUS LIBERTY DOCUMENT*: Ibid, p. 88.

Pg 86. *great men, brave men, the fathers are entitled to the profound gratitude of mankind*: Ibid, p. 63, 224.

Chapter 9 – Speaking the Voice of the Entire People

Pg 89. *But, beyond all these matters*: "Church of the Holy Trinity v. United States, 143 U.S. 457 (1892)," Justia: U.S. Supreme Court, https://supreme.justia.com/cases/federal/us/143/457/.

Pg 90. *There is no dissonance in these declarations*: Ibid.

Pg 90. *These, and many other matters which might be noticed*: Ibid.

Pg 90. *While this case has fallen out of favor in conservative judicial thought*: *Scalia Speaks: Reflections on Law, Faith, and Life Well Lived*, Antonin Scalia, 2017, p 128

Pg 90 *Subsequent cases such as Marsh v. Chambers in 1983*: Justia: U.S. Supreme Court, https://supreme.justia.com/cases/federal/us/463/783/.

Chapter 10 – Showers of Grace

Pg 91. *the whole country was on the very verge*: *The Power of Prayer: and the Prayer of Power*, R.A. Torrey, 2014 (originally published in 1924), p. 244.

Pg 91. *Prayer Meeting from 12 to 1 o'clock*: *The New York City Noon Prayer Meeting*, Talbot W. Chambers, 2002 (originally published in 1858), p. 35.

Pg 92. *HOW OFTEN SHALL I PRAY?*: Ibid, p. 36.

Pg 92. *Depend on Him, thou canst not fail*: Ibid, p. 36.

Pg 93. *Seeing the intense spiritual hunger*: *The Great Prayer Awakening of 1857-58: The Prayer Movement that Ended Slavery and Saved the American Union*, Eddie L. Hyatt, 2019, p. 21.

Pg 94. *A ship was docked in New York Harbor*: Ibid, p. 24, 26, 29.

Pg 94. *I came from India, and I landed but yesterday*: *The New York City Noon Prayer Meeting*, Talbot W. Chambers, 2002 (originally published in 1858), p. 51.

Chapter 11 – With That Assistance We Could Not Fail

Pg 97–98. *My friends – no one, not in my situation*: "Farewell Address," National Park Service: Lincoln Home National Historic Site, https://www.nps.gov/liho/learn/historyculture/farewell.htm.

Pg 98. *Intoxicated with unbroken success*: "H.Res. 597 (106th): Reaffirming the proclamation signed by President Abraham Lincoln on March 30, 1863, in which President Lincoln called for national humility, fasting, and prayer, and for other purposes," GOVTRACK.us: Tracking Congress & the White House, https://www.govtrack.us/congress/bills/106/hres597/text.

Pg 98. *I have been driven many times to my knees*: "Abraham Lincoln Quotes," AbrahamLincoln.org, https://www.abrahamlincoln.org/features/speeches-writings/abraham-lincoln-quotes/index.html.

Pg 98–99. *We have been the recipients of the choicest bounties of Heaven*: "Proclamation 97 – Appointing a Day of National Humiliation, Fasting, and Prayer," The American Presidency Project: Abraham Lincoln, https://www.presidency.ucsb.edu/documents/proclamation-97-appointing-day-national-humiliation-fasting-and-prayer.

Chapter 12 – Completing the Circuit

Pg 101–102. *This is your book: Strength for Service to God and Country (Introduction)*, Ed. Norman Nygaard, 1942.

Pg 102. *There comes a time: And Then They Prayed: Moments in American History Impacted By Prayer*, Barry Loudermilk, 2011, p. 152.

Pg 103. *Almighty and most merciful Father*: "The True Story of 'The Patton Prayer,'" The Imaginative Conservative, James Hugh O'Neill, March 24th, 2022, https://theimaginativeconservative.org/2022/03/true-story-patton-prayer-james-hugh-o-neill.html.

Pg 103–104. *Chaplain, I am a strong believer in Prayer*: Ibid.

Pg 104. *I wish you would put out a Training Letter on this subject*: Ibid.

Pg 104. *The approval, the encouragement, and the enthusiastic support* and *on the importance of prayer*: Ibid.

Pg 105. *Those who pray do more for the world than those who fight*: *And Then They Prayed: Moments in American History Impacted By Prayer*, Barry Loudermilk, 2011, p. 63.

Pg 105–106. *Urge all your men to pray* and *Well Padre*: Ibid, p. 64.

Pg 106. *Doss prayed!*: "Corporal Desmond T. Doss – The WWII Hero who never fired a shot," History of Sorts, https://dirkdeklein. net/2016/07/30/corporal-desmond-t-doss-the-wwii-hero-who-never-fired-a-shot/.

Chapter 13 – A Message Worth Sending

Pg 107. *We are now approaching lunar sunrise*: "Apollo 8 – Christmas Eve 1968," University of Kansas, https://www.ittc.ku.edu/~evans/aviation/apollo8/.

Chapter 14 – The Rock On Which Our Republic Rests

Pg 109–110. *Whereas the Bible, the Word of God has made a unique contribution*: "S.J.Res.165 – A joint resolution authorizing and requesting the President to proclaim 1983 as the 'Year of the Bible,'" Congress.gov, https://www.congress.gov/bill/97th-congress/senate-joint-resolution/165/text.

Pg 111–112. *Of the many influences that have shaped the United States of America*: "Proclamation 5018 – Year of the Bible, 1983," The American Presidency Project, https://www.presidency.ucsb.edu/documents/proclamation-5018-year-the-bible-1983.

Chapter 15 – Regardless of Mere Manpower

Pg 118. *Duty is ours, results are God's*: "DUTY is ours; results are God's" – American Minute with Bill Federer, July 29, 2023, https://americanminute.com/blogs/todays-american-minute/duty-is-ours-results-are-gods-american-minute-with-bill-federer.

Pg 118–119. *In the mid-1950s, the track and field world was awash*: "Four-minute mile," Wikipedia, https://en.wikipedia.org/wiki/Four-minute_mile.

Pg 119. *One cannot measure manpower by counting troops*: *Strength For Service to God and Country (Oct 4)*, Ed. Norman Nygaard, 1942.

Chapter 16 – Words of Faith That Save a Nation

Pg 123–124. *I took Jesus as my Savior on a night not long ago*: "Never Let a Chance Go By," Kenneth Parker, 1973.

Chapter 17 – Living the Motto

Pg 131. *It takes more like 60-254 days to solidify it*: "How Long Does It Really Take to Form a Habit?" *Scientific American*, Jocelyn Solis-Moreira, January 24, 2024, https://www.scientificamerican.com/article/how-long-does-it-really-take-to-form-a-habit/.

Chapter 18 – Engraved

Pg 135–136. *My own feeling in the matter*: "ROOSEVELT DROPPED 'IN GOD WE TRUST'; President Says Such a Motto on Coin Is Irreverence, close to Sacrilege, NO LAW COMMANDS ITS USE He Trusts Congress Will Not Direct Him to Replace the Exalted Phrase That Invited Constant Levity," *The New York Times*, November 14, 1907, https://www.nytimes.com/1907/11/14/archives/roosevelt-dropped-in-god-we-trust-president-says-such-a-motto-on.html.

Pg 138. *Hoped the Lord was on our side*: *Illustrated Life, Services, Martyrdom, and Funeral of Abraham Lincoln*, "Bishop Simpson's Funeral Oration," Delivered May 4, 1865, p. 252.

Pg 145–146. *His enemy, his ancient foe*: https://www.youtube.com/watch?v=YB8CzH4UuqI.

Chapter 19 – Is God Dead?

Pg 148. *Is God dead?*: "Sojourner Truth challenged Frederick Douglass," UMI, https://urbanministries.com/sojourner-truth-challenged-frederick-douglass/. Also in *Sojourner Truth: A Life, A Symbol*, Nell Irvin Painter, 1996.

Pg 151. *used to say that something MUST happen*: *The Britannica Dictionary*, https://www.britannica.com/dictionary/if.

Chapter 21 – NO!

Pg 157–158. *It's out of your hands, you've done all you can do*: "Look to God: Is Anything Too Hard for God?" Marcia Henry, musixmatch, https://www.musixmatch.com/lyrics/West-Coast-Baptist-College/Is-Anything-Too-Hard-for-God.

Chapter 22 – God's Side

Pg 161. *hoped the Lord was on our side*: *Illustrated Life, Services, Martyrdom, and Funeral of Abraham Lincoln*, "Bishop Simpson's Funeral Oration," Delivered May 4, 1865, p. 252.

Pg 162. *The Bible in the hands of Graham's statue*: "Preacher of the Gospel: Billy Graham Statue Unveiled in the U.S. Capitol," The Billy Graham Library, June 13, 2024, https://billygrahamlibrary.org/blog-preacher-of-the-gospel/.

Chapter 23 – A Particular Strength

Pg 165. *triumph of an idea*: Democracy in America and Two Essays on America, Ed. Isaac Kramnick, 2003, p. 43.

Pg 165. *Christianity has therefore maintained a strong sway*: Ibid, p. 497.

Pg 165. *It is religion which has given birth to Anglo-American societies*: Ibid, p. 497.

Pg 166. *In the United States, therefore, it was never intended*: Ibid, p. 85.

Pg 166. *I must say that I have seen Americans making great and sincere sacrifices*: Ibid, p. 595.

Pg 167. *Over a decade ago, Russian President Vladimir Putin made news*: "A Plea for Caution From Russia," *The New York Times*, September 11, 2013, Vladimir V. Putin, https://www.nytimes.com/2013/09/12/opinion/putin-plea-for-caution-from-russia-on-syria.html.

Pg 167. *I have expressed enough to characterize Anglo-American civilization*: Democracy in America and Two Essays on America, Ed. Isaac Kramnick, 2003, p. 55.

Pg 167. *intimately linked together in joint reign over the same land*: Ibid, 345.

Pg 167. *Who is the ultimate sovereign, God or man?*: "The Universal Story," Jonathan Sacks: The Rabbi Sacks Legacy, 9 April 2010, https://rabbisacks.org/archive/the-universal-story/.

Pg 167. *When human beings arrogate supreme power to themselves*: Ibid.

Pg 168. *America is still the country in the world*: Democracy in America and Two Essays on America, Ed. Isaac Kramnick, 2003, p. 340.

Chapter 25 – The Sanction of Our Example

Pg 173. *separation of church and state*: "Jefferson's Letter to the Danbury Baptists," Library of Congress, https://www.loc.gov/loc/lcib/9806/danpre.html.

Pg 173–174. *He went to church … in the U.S. Capitol*: "The State Becomes the Church: Jefferson and Madison," Library of Congress, https://www.loc.gov/exhibits/religion/rel06-2.html.

Pg 174. *Yet, our Founders demonstrated*: Justia: U.S. Supreme Court, https://supreme.justia.com/cases/federal/us/572/565/.

Chapter 26 – Our Practices and Our Principles

Pg 177. *This Fourth [of] July is yours, not mine*: *The Speeches of Frederick Douglass*, Ed. John r. McKivigan, Julie Husband, and Heather L. Kaufman, 2018, p. 68.

Pg 178. *The American people, likewise, have made void their law*: Ibid, p. 164.

Pg 178. *GLORIOUS LIBERTY DOCUMENT*: Ibid, p. 88.

Chapter 28 – A Long Road and A Great Desire

Pg 187–189. *Almighty God: Our sons, pride of our Nation*: "Prayer on D-Day," The American Presidency Project, June 6, 1944, https://www.presidency.ucsb.edu/documents/prayer-d-day.

Pg 189. *reflect and do nothing but what duty demands*: "150 YEARS AGO, NATHAN HALE DIED FOR HIS PEOPLE," *The New York Times*, R.I. Duffin, September 26, 1926, https://www.nytimes.com/1926/09/26/archives/150-years-ago-nathan-hale-died-for-his-people-his-last-words-i.html.

Pg 190. *sensible and spirited speech.* "When Youth Were Patriots: 21-year-old Nathan Hale 'I only regret that I have but one life to lose for my country!", American Minute with Bill Federer, February 25, 2024, https://americanminute.com/blogs/todays-american-minute/when-youth-were-patriots-21-year-old-nathan-hale-i-only-regret-that-i-have-but-one-life-to-lose-for-my-country-american-minute-with-bill-federer.

Pg 190. *I only regret that I have but one life to lose for my country*: *Life of Captain Nathan Hale: The Martyr Spy of the American Revolution*, I.W. Stuart, 1856, p. 134.

Pg 190. *Was I in your condition*: *Documentary Life of Nathan Hale*, George Dudley Seymour, 1941, "Nathan Hale From His Classmate Benjamin Tallmadge," July 4, 1775, p. 39, https://archive.org/details/documentarylifeo00seym/page/36/mode/2up.

Pg 190–191. *Disturb us, Lord*: *Black People Can't Swim: Finding the Faith to Defy Your Odds*, Damone Brown, 2024.

Pg 191. *I am not afraid to go*: "The Death of George Washington," George Washington's Mount Vernon, https://www.mountvernon.org/library/digitalhistory/digital-encyclopedia/article/the-death-of-george-washington.

Pg 191. *Tis Well*: George Washington's Mount Vernon, https://www.mountvernon.org/library/digitalhistory/past-projects/quotes/article/tis-well.

Pg 192. *I am the resurrection and the life*: Washington used a slightly modified version of John 11:25-26 on his tomb "Tomb of George Washington – interior inscription – Mount Vernon," Wikimedia Commons, https://commons.wikimedia.org/wiki/File:Tomb_of_George_Washington_-_interior_inscription_-_Mount_Vernon.jpg.

ACKNOWLEDGEMENTS

We want to begin by thanking our Lord and Savior, Jesus Christ, for all His mighty and manifold blessings. He is ultimately trustworthy – in our lives, for our nation, and throughout eternity.

We also want to profoundly thank Team Wells and Team Teichert. It is a true joy to serve together in Washington, D.C. through GraceWay Baptist Church for such a time as this.

We deeply appreciate those who substantially shaped this book throughout the writing process. We are thankful to Jessica Marshall for her masterful help in molding this book into a quality final product poised for maximum impact. We are also thoroughly grateful for Jeremy and Alyssa Lofgren for crafting an ideal cover design and creating a wonderful overall format. We are also thankful for the incredible recommendations and thorough sanity check provided by Dave Lewin, Caleb & Juliana Walker, Levy Pait, and Jerry Dunwoody.

In this year of our nation's semiquincentennial (our new favorite word), we humbly offer this book to our fellow Americans. It is timely, it is revelent, and it is carefully designed to help wrestle our nation back to where it belongs … a land characterized by strong and enduring trust in the Lord our God! We echo the statement of our current Speaker of the House, Mike Johnson, "America is great, distinct, and exceptional because we acknowledge our motto – 'In God We Trust.'"

May this year be one of revival, where we each make the national motto our *personal declaration*.

ABOUT THE AUTHORS

BRIGADIER GENERAL JOHN "DRAGON" TEICHERT
United States Air Force (retired)

After graduating from the Massachusetts Institute of Technology and Stanford University, John entered the United States Air Force as an F-15E combat pilot. He would go on to serve as an F-22 test pilot and eventually lead as the commander of Joint Base Andrews, the commander of Edwards Air Force Base, and our nation's Senior Defense Official in Iraq. General Teichert ended his service in the Air Force as the Assistant Deputy Undersecretary of the Air Force, International Affairs. During his career, he logged over 2,000 flight hours in 38 different aircraft types.

General Teichert is a champion for inspirational, innovative, integrity-filled leadership. He has vast whole of government leadership experience – from cutting-edge technology to our nation's most sensitive international relationships. John writes and speaks extensively on leadership, innovation, advanced technology, national security, and international affairs. He is an Amazon #1 best-selling author and a former candidate for U.S. Senate who maintains a robust schedule of high-level media engagements. John is also the founder and president of Capital Leadership LLC, intentionally developing the leaders our nation needs and fostering a leadership style that breaks barriers, challenges convention, and ignites innovation.

John has a deep burden for our nation to return to its foundational principles. He was saved by grace through faith in Christ in 2004, and eagerly seeks opportunities to serve the Lord. He is the founder of the PLUS ministry (Prayer at Lunchtime for the United States), and enjoys opportunities to preach around the world.

General Teichert's varied activities can best be followed through johnteichert.com, prayatlunch.us, and LinkedIn as he continues to serve with his amazing wife Dr. Melonie Teichert and their three remarkable children. He passionately and tirelessly strives to maximize his impact on people and our nation for the Lord.

PASTOR BRAD WELLS
GraceWay Baptist Church, Washington, D.C.

Brad was born in Los Angeles, CA to aspiring missionaries, Dennis and Dee Wells. After a year in Bolivia, his parents returned to the States to build a home and help strengthen local churches in California, Colorado, and Idaho.

When Brad was 18, his dad revisited his former aspiration, taking his family of five to the jungles of Papua New Guinea as full-time missionaries. It was on this remote island where Brad surrendered his dream of becoming a millionaire before the age of 30 and answered the call to reach the people of Papua New Guinea with the Gospel of Jesus Christ.

Upon completing his bachelor's degree in theology, Brad met and married his wife Deborah. Together they served with their seven children in Papua New Guinea from 1997 to 2014. They established two churches, a Bible college, and the country's first Christian radio station.

In 2013, Brad began to sense a new leading in his call. He prayed earnestly for direction and heard a distinct answer from Jonah 1:2,

"Arise…go…cry against that great city." Through counsel, confirmation, and commissioning, God led Brad and his family to Washington, D.C. in July of 2014. GraceWay Baptist Church was founded on January 11, 2015, and under Brad's leadership, it has grown into a vibrant community of faith that is making a difference on Capitol Hill. In 2025, God opened the way for GraceWay to acquire their own building in Eastern Market, just seven blocks from the U.S. Capitol.

For his service at home and abroad, Brad was awarded an honorary doctorate degree by his alma mater in July of 2025. Brad has been a spiritual advisor to many members of Congress and their staffs for over a decade. He conducts weekly Bible studies in both Congress and at the White House; and, beginning with Speaker Paul Ryan, serves as a congressional chaplain to leadership.